MASTERING THE STEPS TO SUCCESS:

Achieving Success at Every Rung

Proven Strategies for Overcoming Obstacles and Reaching Greatness. Develop, Learn, Succeed

CHRÍO ZOË

CONTENTS

ACKNOWLEDGEMENT

Writing this book has been a labor and a journey that I couldn't have undertaken without the incredible support and encouragement of many individuals. I am profoundly grateful to all those who have played a part in bringing this project to fruition.

I would like to thank each person who was instrumental in shaping my path to "Mastering the Steps to Success." My sincerest appreciation goes to the countless friends and family who graciously gave me space and time to make this book become a reality.

First and foremost, I want to express my deepest gratitude to my family whose unwavering belief in me and constant encouragement have been my driving force. Your love and support have sustained me through the challenges of this creative process. I give honor to my late parents, whose unwavering belief has been the catalyst to propel me in this journey. Their constant encouragement and unconditional love have been my strength to pursue this endeavor. I say thank you to my siblings Michael, Anthony, Pauline and Sharon who have now passed on but are the silent voices that ignited me to write this book. Through their life, in their own small contributing way, I have come to realize that this journey we call life is valuable and how we start the journey does not dictate how we finish it.

I would like to thank all of my mentors and teachers who helped me by sharing their invaluable knowledge base with me, as they guided me from a place of knowing in shaping my ideas and refining my writing. I cherish your warm guidance, encouragement, and belief in me, and my potential and I can attest to the fact that it has been transformative. I am sincerely hoping that this book will serve as a helpful resource and companion guide on my readers' journey toward self-improvement, empowerment, and fulfillment.

I'd also like to thank the team at AIA for their dedication and hard work in bringing this book to life. Your expertise and guidance in outlining, design, formatting, and marketing have been pivotal in turning my manuscript into a polished publication.

Additionally, I am grateful to my dear friends, who provided much-needed moral support and encouragement during the writing process. I am forever grateful for your influence and for your push to encourage me into what you believe I could be. Thank you all for the guidance and the wisdom you shared with me as I stumbled along my sometimes-rocky road of personal growth and self-discovery. I extend my heartfelt appreciation to my friends and colleagues who provided valuable feedback, engaged in insightful discussions, and cheered me on during moments of doubt. Your enthusiasm has been contagious and uplifting.

Finally, I want to acknowledge my readers—those who will engage with this book. Your curiosity and interest in my ideas fuel my passion for writing, and I hope this book resonates with you in meaningful ways. In writing this book, I've come to realize that the journey is made sweeter by the presence of supportive souls. To all those I've mentioned and to anyone whose name might have been inadvertently omitted, please know that your impact has been immeasurable.

To all of you, your enthusiasm, engagement, and support to me have been more than appreciated. Let me end by saying once again to my readers that I applaud you for buying this book to enhance and empower your personal development. I trust that this book will meet your desire.

With heartfelt thanks,

Chrío Zoë

INTRODUCTION

WHAT THIS BOOK IS ALL ABOUT

Hey friend,

Are you ready for a journey that could change your life? Come join me as I teach you how to master success and achieve it at every stage of life. Together, we'll explore ways to achieve fulfillment and accomplishment in all aspects of our lives. I'm genuinely excited to be alongside you on this adventure.

In a world of dreams and ambitions, success serves as a guiding light that leads us towards greatness. It's the destination that captures our imagination and motivates us to live purposefully. So, what does true success really mean? Is it about accumulating wealth? Is it about being a millionaire or a billionaire? Is it about being famous? Or is it something else entirely?

Achieving success in today's paced and ever-changing world may seem daunting. It's natural to question whether we possess the knowledge, skills, and mindset to thrive. However, let me assure you that reaching success is not a pipe dream. It's a journey for anyone to embrace the right principles and take deliberate steps forward.

I firmly believe that the concept of *"success"* holds significance regardless of our backgrounds. Within this book, you'll discover a roadmap to navigate your path toward success.

Whether you dream of becoming a business owner, an employee, a dedicated student, or simply someone who wants to improve their life, this book will provide you with the tools and knowledge to accomplish your goals. So, how will we make it happen? Well, we're about to embark on a journey.

Throughout this journey of self-discovery, we'll explore the elements that contribute to a life. Each chapter ahead will offer insights into success from different perspectives. To begin with, we'll debunk misconceptions about what defines success. Then, we'll dive into the foundations of achievement and how they shape our perception of ourselves and our capabilities.

As our journey progresses, we'll lay the groundwork for cultivating a mindset that fosters resilience, determination, and unwavering belief in our abilities. You'll gain a perspective on failure as a stepping stone towards achieving success.

Armed with this newfound outlook on life, you should now focus on setting objectives that align with your values and aspirations. I have designed this book to empower you with the knowledge that you can use to develop a mindset that leads to success. I am not going to hold anything back from you, and the hard truth about success is that you need to have the right attitude. An attitude where you seek continuous growth and development.

As you navigate through the realm of achieving your goals, you will come to realize the importance of having a network. A community of individuals who uplift and inspire you to become the best version of yourself. Throughout this book, you'll also learn why it's important to seek out role models. You'll learn that a role model is a person who's more than just an inspiration. A role model is someone we admire, someone we can learn from, someone who knows success, and looking at them just reminds us that we're not alone in the pursuit of greatness.

As this transformative journey comes to an end, you will emerge equipped with the knowledge, skills, and unwavering determination required for success. This book is filled with steps and invaluable advice that can truly make a difference.

However, it's crucial to understand that success is not a destination but an ongoing voyage where consistent effort must be invested. Remember that true greatness is not solely achieved at the end of this path but lies within the experiences encountered along the way.

By delving into the wisdom shared within these pages, you will find yourself guided towards the life you have always envisioned. Along your path, you will inevitably face hurdles, challenges, and moments of uncertainty. Worry not! This book has been specifically crafted to equip you with the resilience and strategies needed to overcome any adversities that may arise. You learn that it is through perseverance, adaptability, and unwavering determination you can indeed reach the triumph you seek.

Before we move forward, it's important to emphasize that success encompasses more than achievements. It also involves finding fulfillment and happiness and developing a deep sense of purpose. By mastering the steps outlined in this book, not only will you achieve success in your chosen endeavors, but you'll also experience true contentment and satisfaction throughout your life.

My friend, I once again invite you to embark on a journey. Together, you and I will talk about how to embrace the challenges and seize the opportunities that lie ahead of us. Success awaits at every step of our voyage, and with sheer dedication and commitment, we can indeed reach new heights.

Are you ready to take the leap? Do you feel a certainty within yourself to dive into this adventure? Yes?

Come with me as we uncover the wonders that lie ahead on the path to success. Let's embark on a voyage towards a triumphant life. May this book become your trusted companion, providing motivation and guidance as you ascend the ladder of success.

With enthusiasm and eager anticipation

Chrío Zoe

CHAPTER 1

UNDERSTANDING SUCCESS

"WHAT DOES IT MEAN TO ACHIEVE SUCCESS?"

Success is a topic that frequently occupies our thoughts and conversations and is deeply ingrained in our society. It serves as a measure of accomplishment and fulfillment. However, when we look at what success means, the definition varies from person to person. Look around you. Some might define success as being rich, while others may define it as having fulfillment that can't be measured using monetary metrics. But have you ever wondered why such variations in the definition of success exist?

The first thing you need to understand is that when we discuss attaining success, it is often associated with reaching our goals and objectives. Being able to do that is seen as an achievement since it's the opposite of failure. However, it's important to know that how we gauge success depends on circumstances and perspectives. Given this, it can be said that what may be considered a victory by one person could be viewed as a loss by another.

Success is often misunderstood. Many individuals believe it is solely tied to material wealth, status, or recognition. However, true success goes beyond these markers. It encompasses growth and satisfaction along with a sense of purpose that extends beyond superficial achievements. Success permeates every aspect of our lives and offers us a state of being.

The experience of success differs for each individual who pursues it. Success transcends norms because what one person deems successful may hold no significance for another. The definition of success varies greatly among individuals as it is influenced by their values, passions, and aspirations.

Have you ever thought about what success means to people?

For some, it revolves around striving for career advancement, achieving their dreams, or reaching the top of their chosen field. These remarkable individuals measure their success by their accomplishments, stability, and recognition for their work. Their unwavering ambition drives them to exceed their expectations and reach heights.

Factors that drive such individuals may include their key performance indicators (KPIs), securing a position further up in the organizational hierarchy, earning a better salary, and more. But these factors aren't drivers or measures of success for those who define it differently.

Did you know that some people find success through relationships? They prioritize building connections. Establishing a support system. Within their families, friendships, and communities, they highly value the love, trust, and harmony they experience. Their satisfaction comes from nurturing relationships, making an impact on others' lives, and finding a sense of belonging.

For these people, simply being with the one they love and seeing them smile is enough for them to know that they're successful. See how different the two definitions of success are. The meaning, the factors, the results, they're all different. What you need to know is that success goes beyond achievements.

It encompasses growth and overall well-being by considering both physical, mental, and emotional health. But that's not all. It involves developing resilience, self-awareness, and having a mindset focused on growth. In this context of success lies the pursuit of learning opportunities for self-improvement while gracefully overcoming challenges with determination.

To achieve success in life, it's crucial to live in alignment with your values and preferences. This means engaging in activities that bring joy and fulfillment while following a path that resonates with your identity—all while making an impact beyond just yourself. Seems like a bit too much, doesn't it? Worry not, dear friend! I'll break it down for you into small bits and pieces so that you'll be able to achieve some dedication and hard work.

Now, let's get down to what success really means!

It's often intertwined with having a sense of purpose, where your actions and endeavors contribute to causes. You might want to improve lives, safeguard the environment, or advocate for justice. Regardless of your purpose, you need to always keep in mind that success is not a destination but an ongoing journey. A journey that's centered on growth, self-reflection, and adaptation. As we go through stages of life, our goals and priorities naturally evolve alongside us.

Think about it. When we're younger, we define success using the aim of owning a Lamborghini or Ferrari one day.

But, as we transition out of those sweet teenage years, the definition of success we have begins to change slightly. Now, we begin to measure success using short-term objectives, with getting into college being the most common one.

Once that's taken care of, our goals change again, and with this evolution of goals comes a change in the definition of success. Now, we decide to label ourselves as successful only if we're able to find a high-paying job. Then, success is about finding your soul mate, settling down, getting married, and starting a family.

Here, the definition of success changes once again. Now, it is also about being a loving and caring parent and spouse and providing for your family. Once your kids are all grown up, success is about paying for their college education and having enough money for your retirement.

But what you need to understand is that success was never about the Lamborghini, the job, the salary, the spouse, or even the kids. Success was about the journey. It was what you did to get the job. It was you using your salary to give to society, it was the time you spent with your loved ones. Beginning to see the full picture here?

Ultimately, the ability to define success lies within you. It's an exploration that requires self-reflection, self-awareness, and the courage to question norms. This personal quest involves contemplating your beliefs, priorities, and aspirations on a level. By embracing your standards of achievement, you can shape a life characterized by authenticity, purposefulness, and profound fulfillment for yourself.

Remember, I said that I was going to break it down for you so you could better understand what success really is? Well, my dear friend, that time is here. To learn what success really means, we need to know that it involves different dimensions.

DIMENSIONS OF SUCCESS

By now, you already know that success is often associated with wealth and fame. However, its true essence goes beyond that. It's a journey that's broken down into different dimensions. So now, let's look at what these dimensions are and how they can shape a fulfilling, meaningful life.

1. **Professional Fulfillment**

This aspect revolves around excelling in one's profession or other vocational pursuits. It encompasses reaching milestones, earning promotions, and receiving recognition for skills and expertise. Professional success not only brings stability but also personal growth and a sense of accomplishment resulting from the contributions one makes to their field.

Ever heard the phrase "growth is a part of success?" Well, this mainly involves gaining knowledge, mastering your existing skills, acquiring new ones, and adopting a mindset that embraces growth and development. Learning and nurturing your intelligence directly influences what you can achieve in life, but it also has an impact on your well-being, which, by all means, is another dimension of success.

2. **Well-being**

Taking care of our health, mental well-being, and emotional balance is a part of finding happiness and overall satisfaction. It's all about prioritizing self-care. But what does that really mean? Self-care is when you learn to manage stress, find balance, and look after yourself. A fulfilling life entails experiencing joy, feeling good about ourselves, and expressing gratitude for what we have.

The goal of trying to be successful is not to beat yourself up! Sure, you have to keep trying and working hard, but draining yourself of all your energy isn't the way to go. I've seen people skip meals, avoid friends and family, and take on stress simply because they're too busy trying to be a "huge success."

But what you need to understand is that this approach only works short-term. It'll take a toll on your physical and mental health soon enough, and before you know it, you'll lose all the motivation and discipline that was driving you toward your goals. Prioritizing your well-being, on the other hand, has the exact opposite effect.

3. **Money**

Money plays a huge role in helping us live our lives the way we want. It opens up opportunities that contribute to our happiness. To achieve success, it's important to handle finances by living within our means and establishing a foundation that supports both personal and professional aspirations.

However, handling personal finances is a concept that is often misunderstood by many. You see, most people just think that if they have enough money to take care of their needs and wants, they're good to go. This might be the essence of managing personal finances, but there's more to it than just that.

Effectively managing your personal finances entails that you should have enough money to take care of whatever it is you need to take care of. But it also means that you need to make your money work for you. This basically means saving and investment and can influence our well-being, but we'll get that later on.

The underlying rule for being successful with money is that you need to first divide your income into three categories: expenses, savings, and investment. Every time you generate income, you need to first take care of your expenses. This includes necessities and debts. Then, you need to divide your savings based on three categories: emergency fund, goals, and investment.

Those who manage their finances like this can rest assured knowing that all their expenses are taken care of, they have money saved up for a rainy day, and some profitable investments. Having such certainty can help you remove stress from life and allow you to find true meaning and fulfillment.

4. Relationship

Developing connections with others adds to our sense of fulfillment. Developing and nurturing relationships with family, friends, colleagues, and the community gives us a sense of belongingness while offering support. This idea of achieving success revolves around the importance of communication skills in meeting the needs of others and building interpersonal relationships.

Knowing you can achieve your dreams is a great feeling, but if you can help others do the same feels even better. And that's what success is all about. Remember, you not only need to work on yourself, but you also need to develop and foster relationships with those close to you so you can be the light in the darkness for them.

5. Contributions

By utilizing our skills and resources, we can make an impact on the lives of others and society as a whole. This could involve acts of kindness, engaging in community service activities, or providing assistance to those in need. Not only does this bring meaning and fulfillment to our lives, but it also leaves a lasting legacy beyond personal achievements.

This might sound a bit cliche, but giving back is a huge part of being successful. When you embark on your journey to success, you'll soon realize that the road isn't smooth. Being successful doesn't mean that you have what it takes to complete your journey, regardless of the conditions. It means that you have what it takes to make the road better for those who follow in your footsteps.

6. Spirituality and Inner Fulfillment

This aspect explores the connection with ourselves through spirituality, uncovering a sense of meaning and purpose in life. To thrive in this world, individuals often engage in practices such as meditation, reflecting on their existence and aligning their actions with their values and beliefs.

I have seen so many people who have it all in life. The car, the house, the kids, the family, the money, everything. Despite this, they're always looking to do something that can help them fill the gap inside. They always have that "something" which keeps them up at night. In most cases, I've found that the "something" is the lack of a spiritual connection with oneself.

7. Achieving Work-Life Balance

A key to living a fulfilling life is finding an equilibrium between work responsibilities and personal well-being. Striking this balance allows people to excel both professionally and personally while preventing burnout and promoting happiness. It doesn't matter whether you have a job or run your business. You don't want to be trapped in the office all day.

To live a truly fulfilling life, you need to have time to work. However, you also need to have time for your passion, hobbies, and family and friends. Fulfillment doesn't come from work alone. It comes from developing and maintaining a fine balance between all the things that are going on in your life.

8. Overcoming Challenges and Building Resilience

Accomplished individuals face setbacks and failures. This aspect highlights the ability to confront obstacles, learn from mistakes, and persevere despite outcomes. Successful individuals incorporate these experiences into their journey toward accomplishments. I'm sure that you've heard the saying *"the road to success is paved with failures"* or something similar.

Trust me when I say that is indeed true. Successful people don't let challenges and setbacks derail them. Instead, they use each challenge and failure as a lesson they can learn something from. Those who use this approach are able to see and categorize failure as a list of don'ts that they can avoid while in pursuit of their goals.

True success extends beyond one's lifetime by leaving an enduring impact on others or society as a whole. Establishing a legacy through one's work, beliefs, and contributions ensures that their success goes beyond their time and continues to make a difference for generations to come.

CHALLENGING MISCONCEPTIONS ABOUT SUCCESS

Throughout history, there have been myths surrounding success, a topic that has always fascinated people. The pursuit of success often intertwines with ideas of happiness, wealth, and achievement. However, there are misconceptions that can cloud our understanding and make it difficult to truly grasp what success really means. In this narrative, let's explore what some of these misconceptions are.

Success is solely determined by luck.

It is often believed that achieving success is simply a matter of being incredibly lucky or being in the right place at the right time. While luck may play a role at times, success is the result of one's efforts, determination, and resilience. Reaching one's goals requires years of work and overcoming numerous obstacles.

Success happens overnight.

The media often portrays success as something that happens instantly for individuals who seem to achieve greatness within a period of time. However, this portrayal fails to acknowledge the reality that significant accomplishments rarely occur with one stroke of luck.

Achieving success requires dedication, continuous learning, and the ability to adapt to changing circumstances. It's common for us to idealize these *"successes"* without considering the years of work and setbacks that come with them.

Success is a destination.

Many people tend to view success as a destination, a peak where we reach and find fulfillment. But in reality, success is not a fixed endpoint; it's a journey. It involves striving for self-improvement and personal growth while appreciating every milestone we achieve along the way. As individuals, our understanding of what success means evolves over time.

Having everything figured out defines success.

Have you ever wondered if successful people have their lives completely figured out? I used to believe that until I realized that bouncing back from setbacks and learning from mistakes is actually more crucial than having all the answers. Successful individuals embrace uncertainty. They are always seeking ways to enhance themselves and their work.

Success is solely measured by wealth.

Success can be measured beyond material riches. It encompasses expanding our horizons, building connections with others, making an impact on the world, and finding contentment within ourselves. It's important to understand that true happiness and success require acknowledging and nurturing aspects of our existence.

Success is not limited to a few.

Some individuals hold the belief that only those who possess talent or luck can achieve things. This misconception often discourages others from pursuing their passions. However, the truth is that anyone can attain success if they are willing to dedicate time and effort, remain focused, and make sacrifices.

Success does not mean avoiding failure.

In reality, setbacks and failures are inevitable on the path to success. They actually play a role in helping us become more resilient, teaching us lessons, and revealing areas where we can improve. True success lies in embracing setbacks as opportunities for growth rather than viewing them as obstacles.

Success does not guarantee happiness.

While achieving success may bring moments of joy, it does not ensure a lifetime of unending happiness. Happiness is complex and ever-evolving, making it impossible to manufacture artificially. Instead, genuine and enduring happiness stems from finding contentment in our pursuits, expressing gratitude for what we have, and nurturing relationships with others. These pillars serve as the foundation for lasting happiness.

By dispelling these misconceptions about success, we can develop a perspective on achieving our goals. Continuously seeking knowledge, adapting to situations, and investing time and effort are components of any successful endeavor. With perseverance and an understanding of what matters in life, we can lead fulfilling lives.

Alright, so now that we know what success really means and have broken it down into different dimensions, we're in good shape to get in the headspace for success. In the next chapter, we'll focus on the psychological side of success and how we can develop the right mindset.

THE PSYCHOLOGY OF SUCCESS

Developing a mindset oriented towards success and maintaining an outlook can have an impact on various aspects of your life and overall achievements. Believe it or not, your mindset plays a role in growth, resilience, and effectively navigating challenges. If you want to truly master success, you need to understand the psychology behind it.

This is something that's easier said than done most of the time. When it comes to the physiological aspect, most people just stop with the understanding that "I think I can make it, I'll make it." However, that right there is just the tip of the iceberg. What you need to know in your pursuit of success is that the physiological aspect of it is divided into various attributes.

Such attributes often include a mindset that's centered around growth, setting achievable goals, and nurturing gratitude. Before we dive deep into the details of these attributes, you need to know that by cultivating them, you can enhance your success in every aspect of your life. This includes your career, relationships, spirituality, personal development, and more.

So, with that in mind, let's look at what these attributes are in more detail.

1. The Mindset

You need to embrace a mindset that focuses on growth by releasing fixed thinking patterns. When you walk through life with a fixed mindset, you basically believe that things like your talent, intelligence, and skills can't be changed. A severe drawback of this mindset is that it leads you to avoid change.

Whenever circumstances challenge that limit of your current capabilities, instead of facing those circumstances, you deviate. However, a growth mindset is one that entails that your talent, intelligence, and skills are things that you can nurture and improve with time and effort. Such a mindset empowers you with the ability to adapt to evolving with changing circumstances and prevail with the desired results.

That said, you need to believe in the potential to enhance your abilities and intelligence through perseverance and effort. Instead of perceiving obstacles or setbacks as roadblocks, you need to see them as opportunities for growth and learning. Remember, you need to remain open to experiences and feedback and commit yourself to self-improvement.

2.   **Your Goals**

The next attribute that makes up the psychology of success is setting achievable goals. It's important for you to know that when you think about setting big goals like starting a million-dollar business, the initial thought that comes to mind negates the idea. This occurs because the end result is often too far to see.

However, this can be fixed by setting achievable goals. What this means is that you need to break down your goals into small steps you can work towards on a daily basis. This approach will help you define your goals into smaller targets and will keep you focused, motivated, and empowered with a sense of purpose on a daily basis.

3. Gratitude

Nurture gratitude by dedicating a moment each day to reflect on the things you're grateful for, no matter how big or small they may be. During times, acknowledging gratitude can shift your perspective. Help you discover the positive elements in your life. Like I said earlier, the road to success isn't smooth.

Oftentimes, the road will break your spirit, and at times, you will lose motivation. It is at those times you'll need to be grateful for all that you have and all that you have done. Being grateful for what you have will acknowledge what is available and what you have at your disposal and will help you make better use of it.

Being grateful for what you have achieved, on the other hand, serves as a sense of achievement and a testament to your own capabilities. This one little act will allow you to realize what you're capable of and will empower you to do so much more. One best practice to show gratitude is to write down all the problems once faced on one side of the paper and tackle them on the other.

The results will surprise you!

4. Your Community

The key attribute to the psychology behind your success is the company you keep. The individuals you choose to surround yourself with can significantly influence your mindset and attitude toward success. If you spend time with people who have a negative mindset, they can poison your mind with similar thoughts.

This soon transitions into demotivation, and then you begin to question your ability to achieve whatever it is you want to achieve. However, the opposite is also true. When you surround yourself with positive people, you begin to embody their qualities. A community of like-minded people can help you improve your current capabilities and prosper.

Therefore, you need to surround yourself with people who uplift and support you.

5. Communication

You need to engage in uplifting conversations. Serve as a source of inspiration for others. When faced with thoughts or self-doubt, challenge them head-on. Replace those beliefs with affirmations whenever they arise. Take time to acknowledge and appreciate your strengths and accomplishments.

Communication is an important aspect of achieving success. You need to have positive communication with both others and yourself. Providing others with inspiration will help you to take a glimpse of the good you can do when you achieve what you desire. In addition, positive communication with yourself will serve as a valuable source of motivation.

6. Learning From Failure

The next and oftentimes the most critical attribute behind the psychology of success is learning. In your pursuit of success, you not only need to acquire knowledge, you also need to learn from failure. View failures as learning opportunities rather than discouraging setbacks.

Embrace your failures and see them as a chance for growth and development. Analyze what went wrong and extract lessons from the experience. Apply that knowledge to make decisions in the future. When you view failure as a learning experience, it will not be a setback for you. Instead, they will serve as a much-needed catalyst for building resilience.

Adopt a mindset that focuses on finding solutions instead of dwelling on failures. Cultivate an attitude that actively seeks approaches to challenges, allowing you to tackle them with optimism and creativity.

7. Responsibility

Taking responsibility for your actions is another critical attribute that helps you in your pursuit of success. Instead of blaming others for your failures and setbacks, you need to take responsibility for them. Developing and living by such a perspective will help you acknowledge that your life is your responsibility.

This acknowledgment will allow you to have more control over your thoughts and actions. It's important for you to understand that when you hold yourself accountable, you automatically become more dedicated and disciplined and put in more effort.

In addition to all of these, you also need to utilize visualization techniques combined with affirmations to boost confidence and motivation in pursuing your goals. Imagine yourself actively engaged in your endeavors while declaring affirmations about your success. Remember, you need first to be able to see yourself achieving success before you can actually achieve it!

I've often found that most people don't quite understand the essence of visualizations and affirmations. They think of these two things as some sort of magic that'll make their dreams come through. If you're someone who thinks like that, I hate to break it to you, but that's not going to happen.

It's important to understand that the goal of visualizations and affirmations is to strengthen your self-image. That's how you see and feel about yourself and can improve your mental and emotional well-being, which are critical aspects of achieving success. In addition, you also need to view obstacles as opportunities that can pave the way toward achieving your goals.

You need to approach challenges with enthusiasm and determination as they provide a chance for growth and accomplishment. Embracing obstacles allows you to open yourself up to possibilities and develop and improve your skills. This proactive mindset leads to progress.

You should also never forget to take the time to celebrate both victories and major achievements along your journey. Recognizing your progress and accomplishments helps reinforce a mindset that keeps you motivated to keep moving.

Above all else, having self-confidence is crucial for maintaining the mindset of believing in your abilities. This helps you improve your perceived worthiness to succeed and increases the likelihood of taking risks, seizing opportunities, and persevering when faced with self-doubt or negative feedback.

BELIEFS AND SELF-DOUBT

I always remember my father's advice; *"To succeed, you must have faith in your abilities and confront any thoughts that hold you back if you want to become unstoppable."* Limiting beliefs are like ingrained patterns of thinking that hinder our potential for success. These self-imposed limitations can prevent us from pursuing our goals and dreams because they reside within our minds.

You need to understand that self-doubt arises when we lack confidence in ourselves or our skills. Many of us carry beliefs about ourselves that we've held since childhood. These beliefs can lead to self-doubt, fear, confusion, and indecision. All of these factors can make it harder for us to achieve success and happiness.

To overcome these challenges, it's necessary to maintain an attitude that compliments constant learning. What truly motivates individuals to take action is their desire for growth and learning in the face of obstacles. It involves recognizing our limiting beliefs and transforming them so that our inner thoughts push us forward instead of holding us back.

When I realized there were areas where I needed to improve my skills, it filled me with optimism and opened doors for development. Understanding this concept is crucial for making progress as it allows you to break free from the chains holding you back.

Remember this truth: Every single person has the ability to rewrite their story. It's truly remarkable that we all possess this power. The words we tell ourselves have an impact. Believe it or not, thoughts like *"I can't do it"* can transform into *"I did it."* True validation comes from within, so it's essential to prioritize what you do. With that in mind, let's explore some ways you can identify self-limiting beliefs.

1. **Engage in self-reflection** - Take time to ponder your thoughts and emotions during challenging moments or when seeking opportunities. Pay attention to any self-talk or thoughts that undermine your confidence. In addition, also make note of what specific events trigger such beliefs.

2. **Take note of recurring patterns and themes** - You are likely to face recurring negative self-talk if you have limiting self-beliefs. By identifying these thoughts, you can recognize areas where you might be placing limitations on yourself.

3. **Reflect on experiences and actions** - Taking note of how you react in such circumstances can help shape

your perspectives. This includes acknowledging mistakes, criticism received, or rejections that have influenced how you see yourself.

4. **Seek input from those you trust** - Consult with your friends, family members, or teachers. Ask for their insights and valuable feedback to gain a perspective on how your own thoughts and uncertainties may impact your decisions and actions.

OVERCOMING SELF-DOUBTS

Remember that ideas can be flexible and modified according to our desires. However, it's important to acknowledge that this process may require effort. With dedication and self-awareness, you can navigate through these changes successfully. Now that you've understood how you can identify self-limiting beliefs and self-doubt, the next thing you need to learn is how to overcome these beliefs.

To do this, the first thing that you need to do is to take the time to organize your surroundings. Believe it or not, they can greatly influence your beliefs. This might seem a bit odd, but maintaining a spacious environment can have an impact on your well-being and help foster more optimistic thinking. So, what you need to do is declutter both your home and workspace to create an atmosphere of clarity.

You can even consider rearranging the layout of your space to improve its flow. Embracing minimalism is a way of life that encourages letting go of limiting beliefs and embracing clarity and honesty instead. When you adopt a minimalist lifestyle, you declutter your environment from anything and everything that doesn't serve a true purpose.

Think about it: if you frequently find yourself constantly buying clothes, it may be because you have thoughts about your appearance. One possible perspective is that you feel attractive when wearing trendy clothes. Does this really serve a true purpose? Does it bring you one step closer to your goals? Or does this serve as food for your self-limiting belief that states you're not good enough until you're wearing the latest trendy?

Do you ever feel overwhelmed by influences and the clutter of your thoughts? Embracing minimalism can lead you on a journey, empowering you to overcome such pressures. By decluttering your mind and simplifying your life, you can break free from what holds you back and achieve fulfillment.

You won't be bothered by petty concerns such as what others think of your appearance and the way you live. Instead, you'll be able to focus on your goals and objectives with a clear head. This is another thing that can help you be more focused, disciplined, and motivated on your journey to success.

Have you ever wondered what others think or felt curious about exploring ideas? Curiosity opens doors for delving into perspectives and experimenting with concepts. Engaging in conversations with people from different backgrounds is a way to broaden your understanding of the world. This helps increase your knowledge and awareness and allows you to explore opportunities you had never even thought of. Engaging in such pursuits can also help eliminate self-doubt and self-limiting beliefs.

Another thing you do to overcome self-limiting doubts is to improve your meditation practices. As you meditate, examine the origins of your beliefs, which are often influenced by sources that infiltrate our minds. However, if you dedicate one minute each day to meditation, you can take control of your thought process and bring about positive change in your life.

To transform any misguided beliefs, it's important to engage in meditation. This practice allows your mind to declutter and release thoughts. The primary goal of meditation is to let thoughts flow freely without getting attached or interrupted. Doing so helps bring calmness to the mind and helps establish a deeper connection with oneself. As you clear away clutter, you can focus on embracing beliefs that align with your aspirations.

These positive ideas have the potential to replace the negative ones over time. Before you know it, your mind will be filled with empowering thoughts that propel you towards becoming the version of yourself.

Personal growth is about thinking and acting based on ideas that drive self-improvement. It's crucial to invest in ways to grow and develop in every aspect of life. Through self-improvement, we gain an understanding of ourselves. Learn how to overcome our flaws. However, it requires more effort than hoping our limiting beliefs will vanish on their own. Some of the things I like to do to foster my own personal growth include:

- Exploring books written by individuals who share beliefs and perspectives as you do.

- Engaging with podcasts as a source of knowledge and learning for self-improvement.

- Measuring my progress and acknowledging how far I come in setting goals.

- Keeping a journal can be incredibly helpful in tracking growth, especially when it comes to your thoughts and beliefs.

AFFIRMATION & VISUALIZATION

Boosting self-esteem can sometimes be a challenge as it entails embracing qualities about oneself. One effective tool in cultivating self-compassion is using affirmations. By expressing statements about yourself over time, these affirmations have the potential to influence your mindset. For example, if you struggle with believing that you are deserving of love, try writing down *"I am valuable, incredible, and cherished"* on a note or paper.

Gradually, this practice can improve your perception of yourself. Incorporating this routine into your life has the potential to positively impact how you view yourself. This can help you develop an improved self-image and is a great exercise for eliminating self-limiting beliefs and doubts you may have.

When using affirmations, focus on acknowledging your achievements and skills. Utilize these affirmations as reminders of your greatness; they will boost your confidence. Motivate you to push yourself.

Harnessing The Power of Affirmations & Visualization

Utilizing visualization techniques and affirmations is a method for overcoming limiting beliefs and unlocking one's potential. Visualization involves creating images of your desires, while affirmations are statements that boost your self-belief and counteract negative thoughts. By using these techniques, you can reshape your thought patterns by replacing limitations with empowering ideas.

It's important to celebrate every achievement, no matter how small it may seem. Recognizing milestones helps maintain a mindset. Cultivating self-worth is highly beneficial alongside practicing gratitude. In addition, you also need to show compassion towards yourself. You need to treat yourself with the kindness you would extend to a friend.

Remember that making mistakes is a part of the learning process that everyone goes through. It is through learning from our mistakes that we experience growth. It's worth emphasizing that our world is diverse, filled with beliefs that will persist as long as there are different types of people.

However, it's crucial for you to determine which beliefs support you in pursuing the life you've always wanted. Any beliefs that hinder your progress should be overcome so that you can seize the opportunity to create a life beyond your expectations. To do this, you'll need to set goals that directly align with the success you want, but we'll cover all that in the next chapter.

CHAPTER 3

SETTING GOALS FOR SUCCESS

When it comes to setting goals, most people just write down a bunch of things they would like to achieve and label them as their goals. That right there might be the essence of what goal setting is, however, it's all that you need to do. You see, when people set goals that are too broad, they begin to lose focus simply because they have no metric to measure their progress.

But that's not all. Your goals also need to be specific and ones you can actually achieve. Think about it: If everyone had a goal of becoming a millionaire, they work toward that goal for a year or two (maybe more) but would soon quit due to a lack of motivation. Now, you might say to yourself, "Why would that happen?"

Allow me to explain. You see, the goal of becoming a millionaire is too broad. It doesn't really have a time limit or any milestone that could be used to measure progress. So, if they are working towards that goal without milestones, they wouldn't be able to see how far they have come and would not acknowledge their achievements.

This right here would make them feel as if they are not making any progress, and from this point onwards, they'll lose motivation and think the goal is unrealistic. This mindset would then transition into a self-limiting belief and would then hinder their ability to achieve monetary success.

Pretty tricky, isn't it? Well, dear friend, you don't need to worry at all because, in this chapter, I'll teach you all about goals. This includes everything from the actual definition of what a goal is, a goal-setting framework, short and long-term goals, and more. So let's get started.

Understanding Goals

Before we dive into setting goals, you need to understand what a goal really is. However, this can be challenging given that the term is used quite commonly and its actual meaning has deteriorated. Most people often use the word "goals" synonymously with milestones or objectives. However, they're not the same thing, and we'll get into this later on.

Setting defined goals can significantly increase your chances of success regardless of whether you aim for self-improvement, career advancement, or any other aspiration. Now, let's delve into what exactly defines a goal and what it does not entail. Be ready, you might be in for a surprise.

In reality, a goal represents something you strive to accomplish. It reflects your desires or the shared aspirations of a group. A goal signifies your commitment to take action towards achieving the desired results. Simply put, a goal is like a dream that has a deadline attached to it. A goal provides individuals with a sense of direction, purpose, and motivation that keeps them focused on pursuing their dreams.

It is the meaning behind life. It's the purpose you're looking for and, when achieved, gives a true sense of fulfillment. But what you need to understand is that a goal is not just anything that you just want to have simply because it is trendy or everyone else has it. A goal is a desired result that's truly aligned with what you believe your purpose is. It's relevant to who you are, what you can achieve, and the impact you want to have on the world.

A goal serves as your vision for the future. It emerges from contemplation of your personal mission statement, which is all about what you genuinely wish to achieve. Setting time limits for goals is crucial because it adds a sense of responsibility. While most goals require a certain amount of time to achieve, breaking them down into more manageable milestones can help you make progress consistently.

Don't be afraid to set goals that may initially appear challenging. Dream, think outside the box, and propel yourself towards your aspirations. This is something that most people try to do. However, they fail to break these dreams into milestones that are easier to tackle.

To do this, you need to be smart about your goals and need to make sure your goals are SMART as well.

But before we get into that, let's look at the difference between goals and objectives.

GOALS VS OBJECTIVES

It's important to understand that goals and objectives are different things. We already know what a goal is, so now let's look at what objectives are. These are basically the steps or actions you need to take in order to reach your goal, whereas a goal is what you ultimately want to achieve.

For example, saying *"I want to become a speaker"* is stating a goal, while *"By the end of this month, I will work with a coach to improve my public speaking skills"* represents an objective. See how the goal is broad and specifies an end result.

However, the objectives for that goal are more detailed and specify the exact actions you need to take to achieve that goal.

Another important difference is that objectives are short-term and aren't the end result but serve as components for the result. Goals, on the other hand, are long-term achievements that you continue to accumulate throughout your life.

THE SIGNIFICANCE OF ESTABLISHING SMART GOALS

The SMART framework is a great tool you can use to effectively set goals and measure your progress. Using this framework helps you set achievable goals that are bound by time. The SMART framework basically states the goals you set need to be:

- Specific.

- Measurable.

- Achievable.

- Relevant.

- Time bound.

Let's dig a little deeper into each of these aspects and learn more about the SMART framework.

Specific

This aspect of the SMART goals framework is about narrowing down your goals and being as detailed as possible. You need to think of exactly what it is that you plan to achieve and how you plan to achieve it. This allows you to create goals that are crystal clear and helps you maintain focus and motivation.

To make sure that your goals are specific, try answering the five W's. Think about what you want to achieve in life and why it's important to you. But don't just stop there. Also, think about who's involved in your pursuit and who can influence your chances of achieving that goal. It is your boss, the company you work for, your client, your family, or all of them. Remember, you need to be specific.

The next thing you need to do is to determine where it is you need to be located in order to achieve that goal. Think about it for a second: if you want to be at the top of the corporate ladder, you'd ideally need to be in a place that's thriving with businesses so you can avail opportunities.

Lastly, you also need to figure out which factors in your life serve as limitations that keep you from your goals and which serve as resources that can help you achieve them. This might seem like a lot of work at first, but trust me, the results will pay off.

Measurable

The next aspect of the SMART goal framework is about defining metrics that will help you measure your progress. When you measure your progress on a regular basis, you'll be able to see how far you have come. These small achievements will then serve as a source of motivation that is needed to achieve your goals.

In addition, seeing yourself making progress and tracking that progress can also help you develop a positive image and eliminate things like self-doubt and negative beliefs. However, creating measurable goals is a bit tricky though. You can be generic here. You need to set metrics that are precise.

To make your goals more measurable, think about the "How much" or "How many" aspects of the goal. Want to earn more money? How much money? Want to help people? How many people? But don't just stop there. You also need to determine how you'll know you've achieved your goals.

Say your goal was to make a million dollars. However, after making half that amount, you feel fully content. Now, is your goal accomplished, or will you continue to chase money? Are you successful?

Achievable

The next aspect of the SMART goals framework basically states that you need to make sure that your goals are achievable. Catering to this aspect can be a bit tricky. Setting achievable goals doesn't really mean that you go easy on yourself. Remember that your goals should still be challenging.

Most people just set goals that they know they can achieve with minimum effort. However, when they achieve the goal, they don't feel content. That's because they never really experienced any challenges, learned new things, or made any real progress while in pursuit of their goals. They just "achieved" it.

To make sure your goals are achievable, you need to strike the right balance between challenge and comfort. So, to keep it simple, you should be able to achieve your goals with some additional learning and a little more effort than what you put in on a normal day. Another thing you can do is to answer questions like "How do I plan to accomplish this?" or "What factors will restrict me?"

You can also think about whether or not you have the skills and resources that are required to achieve the goal.

Relevant

The next aspect of the SMART goals framework basically states that you need to be relevant. Very few know what that means. Remember, in Chapter 1, we talked about determining what success really means for you. Well, that's where relevance comes from. So, what you need to do here is to ensure that these goals really matter to you.

Trust me when I tell you that is something that can make all the difference in the world. If your goals matter to you, you'll do whatever, and I mean whatever, it takes to achieve them. But, if you set the goal just for the sake of it, you might not be as committed or inclined to achieve it. However, setting relevant goals is that simple.

First, you need to be aware of what success actually looks like for you. Once you have that image in your head, you can begin to ask yourself if the goal is worthwhile and is the right time to start your pursuit of that goal. In addition, you should also consider whether the goals fit your needs or not.

If your answer to all or most of these questions is "Yes," then, dear friend, you've truly found a goal that's relevant to you.

Time-bound

The last aspect of creating SMART goals is to make sure that the goals have a time limit. All that you set for yourself must have a target date or deadline by which you have to achieve them. For most people, having a deadline hanging above their heads might make them feel under pressure.

However, what you need to understand is that the purpose of a deadline is not to put yourself under pressure. The purpose of a deadline is to help you maintain focus and discipline. That said, what you need to do here is set one deadline for the overall goal. Then, a deadline for each objective that propels you towards achieving your goal.

When setting deadlines, it's important that you consider the resources at your disposal and your capabilities. These are the two fundamental factors that influence your chances of achieving goals. Some of your goals may require you to learn a couple of things and upgrade your skill set.

To set effective deadlines, you need to factor in the time required to gain such knowledge as well. Now that you know how to use the SMART framework, let's look at some of the differences between short and long-term goals.

SHORT-TERM VS. LONG-TERM GOALS

In order to set goals, it is crucial to have both short and long-term goals. It's important to understand that each of these targets serves a purpose and possesses distinct qualities. Short-term goals are those that can be achieved within a period, such as a day, a few weeks, or a couple of months. This allows for division into monthly, weekly, and daily targets. Examples of short-term goals include completing a project or course, going to the gym three times a week for a month, or saving a certain amount of money within a few weeks.

On the other hand, long-term goals require time to accomplish and can span several months or even years. Achievable long-term goals may include completing a course, starting a business venture, learning a new language proficiently, or buying a house.

Most people often find differentiating short and long-term goals a bit challenging and overlook the idea altogether. However, you need to know that you can differentiate between these two types of goals using four different factors. Let's look at what these factors are in more detail.

1. **Timeframe** - The main distinction lies in the duration required to achieve each goal. Short-term goals have immediate deadlines and results. However, long-term goals may take months or even years to achieve.

2. **Scope and Specificity** - Short-term goals tend to focus on actions or achievements, whereas long-term goals encompass aspects of life and may not be as specific but are essential to success and fulfillment.

3. **Benefits** - When it comes to setting goals, short-term aspirations provide advantages and a sense of achievement. Conversely, long-term objectives offer enduring benefits that may take time to materialize.

4. **Complexity** - Short-term goals are typically less intricate and can be achieved through small steps. However, long-term goals often involve components that require planning and entail overcoming various challenges.

The pursuit of both short and long-term goals is crucial for growth and success. Striking a balance between the two can keep you motivated, aware of your progress, and satisfied as you work towards your aspirations. In the grand scheme of things, long-term goals provide a sense of purpose and direction, while short-term goals help us remain focused, motivated, and disciplined. Believe it or not, both are equally important for success. So, with that in mind, now let's dive deeper into crafting goals that lead to success.

KEY THINGS TO REMEMBER

Setting goals involves determining what you want to achieve and then devising a plan with steps to reach that point. You or your group commit to a series of desired outcomes or goals that you intend to achieve by a certain deadline.

It's important to understand that to craft goals that lead to success. You must focus on both short and long-term goals. In addition, you also need to define ways that can help you achieve those goals.

When setting goals, it is crucial to be as specific as possible in order to clarify your intentions and determine milestones. For instance, saying *"I want to get in shape "* is the foundation for a tangible goal such as *"I will complete a 5K race within the next six months."*

While it's important to challenge yourself, you need to ensure that your goals are realistically attainable within a timeframe using the resources available. This helps prevent frustration. If a major goal seems daunting, you can always put it down into manageable steps. Defining metrics for tracking progress makes it easier to monitor success and adjust strategies if necessary.

You should also put your goals into writing as it demonstrates dedication and provides clarity. It is essential to keep your written goals visible so that you can review on a regular basis and stay motivated. When you have defined your goals, prioritize them based on their importance and urgency to ensure that your focus remains sharp and that you don't lose motivation.

To better prepare yourself for any obstacles along the way, proactively anticipate them. This is where the SMART goals framework will come in handy. Once you know which obstacles you're likely to face, you need to develop a plan to overcome them. This mental readiness will strengthen your resilience in the face of setbacks and will empower you with the strength needed to overcome them.

Another thing you need to remember is that visualizing the achievement of your goals can boost your confidence. Reinforce your belief in your ability to turn your aspirations into reality through disciplined effort. However, it's important to take action well. Break down your goals into tasks. Dedicate some time every day towards making incremental progress no matter how small it may seem.

Regular self-check-ins are helpful in assessing how close you are to achieving your objectives. Celebrate the milestones while also analyzing areas that need improvement and stay adaptable. Another thing you can do is share your goals with a community that can provide both accountability and encouragement for you to persevere. Additionally, acknowledge milestones along the way with rituals that help sustain motivation and positive habits and propel you in the right direction.

And lastly, when faced with setbacks, avoid labeling them as failures. Instead, view them as opportunities for learning, growth, and refining strategies for success. With that, this chapter comes to an end. Dear friend, I would now request you to take this moment and use this newly acquired knowledge to create your own SMART goals.

Once you've done that, you flip this book open to the next chapter, where we'll talk about how you can master self-discipline.

CHAPTER 4

MASTERING SELF-DISCIPLINE

In the previous chapter, we learned everything we need to learn about goals. One of the key things you've probably noticed throughout this book by now is that to achieve your goals, you need to have unwavering discipline. Believe me when I tell you that discipline is what keeps you going when motivation falls short.

As a child, I have memories of attempting to climb the tree in our backyard. I can still recall those moments when my endeavors fell short. It was a bit painful sometimes. However, there was one day when my grandfather's voice resonated from above as I glanced up at my bedroom window. He said, *"Zoe, first learn to master yourself!"* At that time, his words didn't truly make sense to me.

After hearing that, the first thing I said to myself was, "What is he even talking about? What does he mean to master myself?" Now, honestly speaking, I was a bit too young at that time to truly comprehend what that meant. However, as life went by, I began to realize the true meaning of what my grandfather had said.

So, what you need to understand is that the key to seizing control of your life lies in embracing self-discipline. It's intriguing to witness how self-discipline plays a role in the achievements of individuals who have achieved success worldwide. Take a look around you. Can you name anyone who became successful without putting in the effort?

Most people often have a hard time believing that in life, you get what you put in. So, the more effort you make, the better your results get. What you need to understand here is that the effectiveness of your efforts is indeed tied to your skills but is also influenced by your willingness to use those skills, and that's where self-discipline comes into the picture.

But with that comes the question: *What does self-discipline truly mean?*

Is it about beating yourself up with rules and having no time to enjoy life? Is it about being focused on what truly matters? Is it about creating and following a schedule, or is it something more? I'll give you a textbook definition to start. Self-discipline refers to the ability to regulate one's behavior without relying on motivation or external guidance.

So, what this really means is that you're able to act in a way that propels you toward your goals even when you are low on motivation. When it comes to achieving self-discipline, most people just think that the good old "go hard at it approach" will help them have more self-discipline. However, that's not the case.

What you need to understand is that self-discipline is all about knowing and managing your emotions. Have you ever thought about what happens when you lose motivation? You see, at that time, your energy levels drop, you begin to feel a bit off, and you just want to stop. This moment right here is where your self-discipline is being tested.

Self-discipline is basically your ability to overcome this obstacle of the moment with a sense of purpose and desire for achievement. Practicing self-discipline is essential as it not only helps push you closer to your goals but it also improves your mental and emotional (and, in some cases, physical) well-being.

Self-discipline involves directing your focus toward resisting temptations and persevering toward your goals. It encompasses making decisions that align with long-term objectives despite distractions or challenges. However, my personal definition of self-discipline revolves around the ability to motivate oneself to do what is necessary regardless of inclinations or preferences.

The thing with self-discipline is that it's not as easy to develop as it might seem. Reading about it is one thing, and truly mastering it is another ball game altogether. Now, dear reader, I don't want you to be overwhelmed by this. Mastering self-discipline may be difficult, but I'll share some strategies with you that'll help get the job done. But first, let's focus on understanding the role self-discipline plays in our lives.

THE ROLE OF SELF-DISCIPLINE

The significance of self-discipline in attaining success cannot be understated. There are distractions that can easily pull you away from pursuing your dreams. Constant notifications buzzing on your phone, dishes piling up in the sink, or the inviting comfort of your couch calling out for attention. It's easy to get lost in the chaos of life if you don't have self-discipline guiding you.

Ever thought about what would happen if you made a commitment? Or if you embraced a level of intention and accountability for yourself? If not, then take this moment now to do just that. Take a deep breath and imagine what life you would be like if you had the self-discipline of a monk.

Having self-discipline allows you to evaluate every decision based on your long-term goals and helps you stay focused on the big picture in life. Incorporating routines, such as practicing skills, becomes a part of your routine.

By practicing self-discipline, you consciously choose activities that enrich your life more than everyday entertainment ever could. The ability to resist temptations empowers you to invest quality time with your family, pursue passion projects, and prioritize self-care. Your priorities become crystal clear, and when faced with obstacles, self-discipline gives you the determination to persevere.

At this point, setbacks begin to transform into opportunities for growth. You begin to identify and learn more about the reasons behind you giving up and start to use that knowledge to improve your attitude and behaviors. You begin to push beyond your limit and adapt habits that cultivate resilience and help you achieve your goals.

Procrastination loses its grip on you as self-discipline guides you toward taking action on what matters. You proactively tackle tasks to prevent them from becoming sources of stress and regret. The drive to move forward comes from within you all on its own.

You increasingly take responsibility for your actions by acknowledging both mistakes and accomplishments. This sense of accountability strengthens and then weighs you down. Self-discipline helps shape empowering habits while eliminating time-wasting activities. Rather than surrendering to every passing impulse, you navigate each day with intentionality.

Self-control serves as a guiding force that directs your decisions toward aligning with yourself. By maintaining consistency and demonstrating bravery, you gradually construct the life you have envisioned, one step at a time.

But you need to understand that this journey involves making sacrifices and learning to prioritize what truly holds significance. Nevertheless, self-discipline offers the clarity and resolve required to stay on course. Your aspirations draw nearer with each passing day. With self-discipline as your beacon of guidance, you can achieve the goals you've set for yourself.

So, with that in mind, let's take a look at some of the best strategies you can use to develop self-discipline.

STRATEGIES FOR DEVELOPING SELF-DISCIPLINE

When you have a determination to improve your self-discipline, various opportunities will arise. But what you need to understand here is that willpower alone won't be enough. You need to develop habits of self-discipline and practice them until it becomes your very nature. Before we get into the strategies for self-discipline, there's something else I want you to do first.

Take this moment to reflect on your desires and think about what it is you really want. Money? Peace? Soulmate? Fame? It can be anything. Once you are done with that, think about how to plan to achieve these desires. Now, make a note of all these thoughts rushing through your head.

The thoughts and ideas you need to have about achieving your desires are what can help you cultivate self-discipline. As Napoleon Hill once said, *"Self-discipline begins with gaining control over your thoughts. Without mastering our thinking process, we cannot effectively govern our actions."* Essentially, self-discipline allows us to consider our actions before taking them.

Therefore, it's important to identify what you want from each aspect of your life. Do you need to acquire knowledge about industry trends in order to advance in your career? Are you interested in adopting habits like exercise and healthy living for the purpose of improving well-being, boosting self-confidence, and creating opportunities? What choices are currently available to progress in your field?

What I'm trying to say here is that you need to visualize your aspirations. First, see yourself where you want to be in life. Embody the feelings and emotions that come as a result of this visualization. See your path, plan the steps you're going to take, and embark on a purpose-driven journey.

Regardless of the decisions, take a moment to commit and then start taking action. That right there is the essence of how you develop self-discipline. Now, as promised, I'll share with you some great strategies that'll help you be more disciplined.

1. Identify and eliminate any distractions

It's crucial to recognize and remove any diversions in order to enhance focus and productivity. These interruptions hinder concentration and keep you from making any real progress. Eliminating distractions from your life isn't as easy as it may seem. The trick here is to understand that the desire to pursue a distraction arises from one's inner temptations.

A lot of people might think that they have control over their temptations. But believe me when I tell you that temptations have their own way of sneaking through. Oftentimes, I've found that the most effective strategy for resisting temptation involves minimizing its presence within your surroundings.

If scrolling through your social media feed has become a time-consuming activity for you, there are ways to improve the situation. Let's go into detail using this example since it's become a common problem for most people nowadays. So, the first thing you need to do is consider reducing screen time by setting limits on smartphone usage.

Another thing you can do is put your phone on silent mode or turn those in-app notifications off so you're tempted to check your phone every other minute. You can set specific times dedicated solely to checking your accounts, allowing you to gain control over social media usage.

Lastly, it is worth considering removing any apps from your device that do not align with your goals. You may face challenges when it comes to resisting tempting foods, dealing with people, or overcoming obstacles that hinder your progress. Simplifying your life by reducing distractions will take you a long way from giving in to your temptation. Although it may initially be tough, practicing self-control and saying no to impulsive desires can help you grow and transform into a better version of yourself.

2. **Having someone to hold you accountable**

Accountability can be extremely beneficial when you are working alone and trying to maintain discipline. So you can have someone keep an eye on you in the starting phases. However, you need to make sure that you're picking somebody for the sake of doing it. The person you choose to hold you accountable must understand your goals and purpose.

Above all, that person should have great discipline on their own. This goes without saying, but I'll say it anyway: You don't want to pick a slacker to hold you accountable. Remember, this person should provide you with support and keep you motivated. An accountability partner plays a role in helping you make the necessary changes to control your behavior and make effective decisions.

When you have a goal in mind, the chances of achieving it increase by 10%. However, if you commit to someone about reaching that goal, the probability rises significantly to 65%. If you set a deadline for reporting your progress to that person, the chances soar up to 95%. Knowing that you are accountable not to yourself but to someone else helps maintain motivation as you strive for self-discipline. The same principles apply when supporting others; however, it is crucial that your accountability partner shares the same or somewhat similar objectives.

For instance, if you're looking to acquire a skill, it's beneficial to seek out someone who shares the same goal. To enhance your learning experience further, you may want to consider finding an accountability partner. Together, you can attend classes, study alongside each other, and have discussions about your progress. When selecting a partner, it's important to ensure that both of you are equally committed to growth and discipline.

3. **It's crucial to document your goals.**

Another great strategy that can help you achieve monk-like self-discipline is documenting your progress and goals. Whether you choose to write them down on paper or use a computer, this simple step helps transform your desires into objectives. So go ahead, grab a pen and paper, and start writing, or crack your knuckles and start typing.

Begin by articulating your goals in language. Make everything as detailed and as precise as possible. Remember, effective goals are SMART. They are specific, measurable, attainable, relevant, and time-bound. If you need a refresher on this, you can always go back to the previous chapter. If not, start with milestones while keeping long-term objectives in mind. Setting goals provides visibility. Increases the likelihood of achievement. It also enhances problem-solving skills compared to pursuing objectives that might take longer to accomplish.

As you achieve these milestones one by one, it will fuel your determination and will help you keep pushing forward. For example, if you aim to improve your diet, try gradually introducing one food item each week as opposed to eliminating all unhealthy choices at once.

The small wins you rack up each and every single day will help you build momentum that you can use to truly transform your life. But you must not forget that this here is not a sprint. It's a marathon. By making progress bit by bit, you can train your mind in practicing self-control. This method can help you develop a habit, making it less likely for you to go back to your old ways.

4.   **Create to-do lists**

Another helpful strategy is to outline the tasks required to achieve your goals. Believe it or not, the good old "to-do list" is still the best tool for this. This simple practice keeps you focused and on track, increases productivity, and helps you achieve your goals. Why, you ask? Well, you see, when you write something down, you're more likely to remember it and remain committed to it. Think of it like a contract you make with yourself.

Using reminders in the form of lists can also be beneficial for tracking your progress. When you mark off completed tasks, it instantly motivates you to keep moving. Regularly reviewing your goals ensures that you're heading in the right direction and allows for adjustments, if needed, in terms of specificity, relevance, or achievability without hindering your progress. The key is achieving goals that bring you closer to the life you desire.

Before wrapping up each day, take a moment to make a list for the next day. Cultivating habits like this helps direct your focus toward tasks that improve self-control. Remember to assign dates for all your goals and objectives. This approach will help you stay focused and motivated toward your goals. When you're creating a to-do list, some of the key things you need to remember include:

- Developing a thought-out plan so that everything falls into place smoothly. Start by outlining your steps and then proceed accordingly. Determine which tasks have priority compared to those of importance.

- Grouping your tasks into categories that are related. By performing activities in this way, you will save both time and effort. Not only will this help synchronize your thoughts, but it will also ensure that everything you need is in its designated place.

- Avoiding too many tasks at the same time. Although it may seem like multitasking can increase productivity, it actually hinders focus and mental energy allocation for each task. It's better to tackle one task at a time before moving on to the next.

Remember that progress doesn't always have to be a leap. It's often broken down into steps If accomplishing things seems impossible, start by taking strides towards success. If even that feels overwhelming, simply take steps in that direction. Sometimes, even these small steps can be challenging; don't lose hope. Keep progressing, even if it means advancing inch by inch.

Remember what Martin Luther King said: *"If you find yourself unable to fly, then run. If running is not an option, then walk. If walking becomes difficult, don't hesitate to crawl."* The important thing is to keep moving. Make it a habit to actively work towards your goal at the moment.

The main thing you need to understand is that the pace of your progress isn't what is important; it is the progress itself that matters. It's important to develop time management skills and consistently take actions that bring you closer to success. In order to progress in life, it is crucial to act upon your aspirations.

Based on my research, it has become clear that individuals benefit from creating an *"if-then"* plan that helps them make decisions at any given moment. By anticipating distractions or temptations, you can proactively prepare how you will respond to them. This approach trains your mind to make choices.

But that's not all. The "if-then" approach also facilitates innovative thinking. It allows you to see all the problems before they exist and helps you develop solutions that you may need to use within a moment's notice. To truly master this approach, think about all the possible scenarios that could prevail, how you act or react in each scenario, and would your actions propel you in the right direction.

For example, when a specific situation arises, you can plan ahead with a predetermined response. By following this plan, it is possible to boost self-discipline and foster resilience. This method facilitates growth and enhances your ability to take control of your actions, thoughts, and behaviors.

Practicing self-discipline not only amplifies your capacity to achieve goals but also cultivates a more balanced, purposeful, and fulfilling life. Dear friend, I hope you've found all this information to be of value. I would urge you to incorporate some, if not all, of these things in your life. Trust me, you'll see a difference within weeks.

The initial phases of change will be difficult and come with a few failures. However, you need to embrace these failures and learn to use them to your advantage!

CHAPTER 5

EMBRACING FAILURE AS A STEPPING STONE

Failure is a part of everyone's journey. It doesn't matter who you are; you're going to fail in life at some time. Everyone does, and what you need to understand is that it is better to accept failure than try to avoid it altogether. Accepting failure helps us uncover where we're falling short.

Is it the mindset? The attitude? The skills and efforts? We can get all these answers when we accept the fact that failure is a part of the journey, not the end of the journey. Instead of viewing it as a roadblock, we need to use it as an opportunity to learn and grow. Trust us when I tell you that having the ability to view failure as an opportunity is what sets those who achieve success apart from those who don't.

The hard truth about this is that not everyone has the strength to confront failure head-on, even if they have the mindset and work ethic. However, embracing failure as a transformative experience can turn setbacks into chances for growth and learning while ultimately helping achieve success.

However, this is something that most people don't really understand. Based on my experience, I've found that people don't really know how to perceive failure. But the worst part of this is that they're not really at fault here. You, me, and pretty much everybody else in the world have been taught and conditioned to avoid failure as opposed to learning from it.

UNDERSTANDING THE PERCEPTION OF FAILURE

Jog your memory all the way back to elementary school. All of us have been tested in one way or another since those young years of our lives. From that age, we're taught to avoid the "F" grade. I don't know how they do things in school now, but in that phase of life, if you failed, you were automatically a bad student.

Now, the thing to understand here is that school is the only thing we have going on in our lives at that age. It's pretty much all (at least most) of what we do or are expected to do well at. Failing at the only thing we're expected to succeed in makes us feel like a person, not just a bad student. This thought and emotion then imprints itself on like two magnets clinging together.

But the worst part of all this is that no one ever tells you that it's okay to fail. Everyone just expects us to succeed. From this point onward, we began to do whatever we could to avoid failure. Now, it's important to understand that some of us, at this point, subconsciously begin to tackle failure and this crucial art for becoming successful very early in life, but most don't.

For those of us who don't, we tend to choose options where success is guaranteed, also known as the easy way out. We began to use this approach in almost every decision we make. Fast forward to college, and we only choose majors we know we can pass. We don't really look at whether the chosen field has any value or is sustainable.

When it comes to making career choices, we, again, choose the "safest" option because we don't want failure to define us. There's nothing wrong with this approach. Nothing except for the fact that as we transition through life, the "safe options" become limited. Soon enough, we find ourselves in a position where there are no "safe options," and the only possibilities available to use come with a chance of failure.

It is at this very moment we realize that we never transitioned beyond that elementary school "F" grade. Now, what you need to understand here is that most people in life are taught to avoid failure from a very young age, and those lessons continue to govern our decisions for the rest of our lives.

That right there is the problem we have when it comes to perceiving failure for what it really should be. I give it to you plain and simple: failure is a bad thing on it's not, but not learning from failure is bad. So, instead of avoiding failures and looking for the "guaranteed options," We need to learn how we can embrace failure.

We need to learn how we can constructively acknowledge that we have failed. But we can't just stop there. Once we've acknowledged that we've failed, we need to dissect that failure. We need to see exactly where things started to go downhill. Was it a bad decision? Were the odds stacked against us? Did we not have the right skills? Could we have tried a little bit harder?

After determining the reason, we need to work on it until it no longer serves as a limit but as a strength. All of this is easier said than done, but worry not, dear reader, because towards the end of this chapter, I'll share some great strategies that'll help you embrace failure and learn from it. However, to do that, you must know how to change your perception of failure.

CHANGING HOW YOU PERCEIVE FAILURE

By changing how you perceive failure, you find yourself under the stage lights, tightly holding onto the microphone. You begin your speech with the intention of inspiring the audience. However, your words fall short. Seems to drift until scattered applause breaks the silence in the room.

Despite all the preparation and effort you put in, you encounter failure. This is a moment where you find yourself at a crossroads. Will you perceive this setback as evidence of your shortcomings? Will you see it as a teacher whose lessons can guide you toward success?

How failure impacts you ultimately depends on your perspective. Let's work with this example for a while. If you see this event as a setback, you probably won't get back at all. You'll give in to your passion for public speaking (or whatever else it is you want) and deviate back to your comfort zone.

No lessons learned. No improvement was made. No results and no achievements. Now, let's turn the tables. What if you perceived this not as a setback but as an opportunity for growth? Let me walk you through what would happen if you embrace this failure. To start off, you'd first acknowledge the fact that you've failed, and the failure is your responsibility.

You won't play the blame game. You point fingers and say that the time wasn't right or circumstance had a role to play. Instead, you'll sit back and analyze the moment as you relive it minute by minute. You'll focus on identifying all the things that went wrong. You'll ask yourself questions like, "Was I not confident enough?" "Did I not believe in what I was saying?" "Were my skills not good enough?" and more.

Then, you'll begin to work on yourself. You'll try to figure out how it is that you can build confidence. You'll try to find what's truly meaningful to you so you can believe in what you're saying. You'll master the art of public speaking by continuing learning. You'll grow, you'll improve, and the next time you get on stage, you'll achieve your goals and be fully content with yourself.

See the difference having the right perception can make? Perceiving failure from what you need as an opportunity to learn and grow can take you from a position where you're giving up on your dream to one where you are conquering them day in and day out. I know you've heard the saying "Perception is reality" or something similar to it, at least, right?

Believe me when I tell you that this is indeed true, especially when it comes to failure. Before criticizing yourself, try considering failure as constructive feedback. By analyzing what went wrong, you can gain insights that will help you adjust your approach. Failure should be seen as an evaluation of progress rather than a reflection of your self-worth.

Remember to keep your identity separate from the outcomes. Your failures are a result of what you do. They are not who you are or what you can do. When it comes to changing your perception of failure, you must adopt a growth mindset. This mindset is the key as it acknowledges that skills are developed through practice over time. Setbacks should be viewed as stones on our learning journey. Each failure carries lessons that refine and enhance our abilities.

Rather than fixating on achieving results, try to find joy in the process itself. Acknowledging failure and learning from it can help you unlock a ton of different possibilities. But, first, you must think of failure as the admission fee or success. Developing persistence and resilience comes from overcoming challenges.

Failure teaches us that giving up is never the solution. With determination and perseverance, we can bounce back stronger than before. It is during this journey that we truly uncover our capabilities. It's important to acknowledge and celebrate our achievements just as we appreciate the efforts we put in along the way.

When we encounter setbacks, we should approach them with passion, and that can push us forward. Surrounding ourselves with individuals who see failure as a chance for growth helps us maintain such a perspective. Being part of a community or group where everyone has such a perspective on failures can help us get the extra bit of support we need.

When our plans don't go as expected, curiosity enables us to explore daring paths. Being adaptable is crucial. Think about it for a second: groundbreaking inventions that changed the world often emerged after moments of failure.

Ever imagine what would have happened if Edison had given up on the light bulb?

Setting goals that allow room for learning and personal growth is essential. Mistakes pave the way towards excellence. Progress requires time, effort, and resilience. Failure is a part of success. By embracing wisdom and patience, life's setbacks can be transformed into stones toward realizing our potential. Remember that failure is a part of the journey; it's not the destination.

Now that you're in the headspace for embracing failure let's look at some strategies that can help you see failure as an opportunity for growth as opposed to a dead end.

STRATEGIES FOR EMBRACING FAILURE

Embracing failure is something that varies from person to person. All of us think differently, and therefore, how we see failure is oftentimes not the same. However, what you need to understand here is that the underlying principle of viewing failure as a ladder or a pit never really changes. We can only embrace failure if we choose to see it as a ladder. So, with that in mind, let's look at some key strategies for embracing failure.

1. **Embrace valuable learning opportunities**

   Failure provides us with lessons that success often cannot offer. It encourages us to reflect on our actions, choices, and plans, helping us identify areas for improvement and personal development. Embracing failure allows us to gain insights that can guide our decision-making and future planning.

2. Build resilience and perseverance

These qualities are essential when facing challenges. Failure tests our ability to persist during hard times. When we view setbacks as stepping stones, they teach us how to bounce back and pursue our goals despite adversity. These experiences make us stronger, shape our character, and fuel our determination.

3. Expand comfort zones

Failure can serve as a catalyst for growth by pushing us out of our comfort zones. It encourages us to move beyond our existing knowledge, motivating us to explore unfamiliar territories, take calculated risks, and push the boundaries of what we can do. Embracing the potential for failure unlocks opportunities, fosters our growth, and improves our overall well-being.

4. Embrace innovation and creativity

These qualities often emerge from our experiences of failure. When faced with challenges or obstacles, it is crucial to think and consider solutions. By perceiving failure as an opportunity for growth, we cultivate mindedness and a willingness to experiment with ideas. This mindset can lead us to discoveries and unexplored possibilities.

5. **Developing humility and adaptability**

These two things become a part of our journey when we encounter failure and humble us. They remind us that perfection is unattainable. Failure acts as a teacher that guides us to listen to feedback and make adjustments. To fully embrace setbacks, we must let go of our egos. Recognize our limitations. Then, can we truly learn from mistakes and achieve personal growth?

6. **Redefining success**

This is another outcome of embracing failure. It allows us to redefine our understanding of what success means. This shift in perspective enables us to view success not as the absence of failure but rather as a part of the journey itself. Embracing failure helps us redefine success as the ability to learn, adapt, and persevere in any circumstances.

We've covered quite a lot in this chapter. However, there are a few things that I'd like you to take away with you. You must remember that failure, just like success, is a part of the journey, and it's not the end destination. You also need to remember failure is not what defines us; it's what we do after failure that does.

In your pursuit of success, you'll often find that success is not about never being knocked down. It's about getting back up all the time. Or, as Rocky would say, "It ain't about how hard you Hit. It's about how hard you can get hit and keep moving forward." However, this right here is something that requires building positive habits, which we'll get into in the next chapter.

CHAPTER
"GOOD WILL"

Helping others without expectation of anything in return has been proven to lead to increased happiness and satisfaction in life.

I would love to give you the chance to experience that same feeling during your reading or listening experience today...

All it takes is a few moments of your time to answer one simple question:

Would you make a difference in the life of someone you've never met—without spending any money or seeking recognition for your good will?

If so, I have a small request for you.

If you've found value in your reading or listening experience today, I humbly ask that you take a brief moment right now to leave an honest review of this book. It won't cost you anything but 30 seconds of your time—just a few seconds to share your thoughts with others.

Your voice can go a long way in helping someone else find the same inspiration and knowledge that you have.

Are you familiar with leaving a review for an Audible, Kindle, or e-reader book? If so, it's simple:

If you're on **Audible**: just hit the three dots in the top right of your device, click rate & review, then leave a few sentences about the book along with your star rating.

If you're reading on **Kindle** or an e-reader, simply scroll to the last page of the book and swipe up—the review should prompt from there.

If you're on a **Paperback** or any other physical format of this book, you can find the book page on Amazon (or wherever you bought this) and leave your review right there.

CHAPTER 6

CULTIVATING POSITIVE HABITS

Dear friend, I know that you've probably heard that habits are hard to break, right? But I want to tell you that what you've heard is only half the picture. The other half: they're even harder to build. Over the years, I've found that most people often find it hard to build habits. However, the challenges they face are not all about their ability.

Believe it or not, building habits is a lot more psychological than you might have initially thought it would be. Most people, when cultivating positive habits, don't really understand how they're formed, and the worst part is that they don't even realize that this is what's holding them back.

You see, before you change your behaviors and build positive habits, you first need to understand how they formed. Trust me when I tell you that this will come in handy big time.

When we understand how habits, or anything else for that matter, are formed, we're able to identify both things that can hold you back and things that can propel you in the right direction.

So, with that in mind, let's dig deep into habits and see how they're formed and how you can cultivate them to achieve positive outcomes and propel yourself in the right direction.

UNDERSTANDING HABITS

When it comes to habits, the first thing that you need to know is that habits are formed when behaviors in our lives become automatic and require no minimum conscious awareness. It's a bit of a confusing definition, isn't it? Let's simplify it a bit. You see, habit forms when we don't actively think about what we're doing and do it on the go.

It's like slouching. You don't actively think about it; you just do it once or twice when you are tired at first. One evening, you get home from work, your energy levels are at an all-time low, and you're really tired. You see that couch in the living room that's inviting you. You go and lean back and sit on it. It relieves the pain, gives you comfort, and is just a pleasant experience overall.

At first, it's just a one-time thing. Then, you begin to do it every single time you're tired, and before you know it, slouching becomes a regular habit or a "just the way I sit" type of thing. This right here is how habits are formed. Now, as someone looking to change their negative habits, you need to understand the psychology in the example above.

There's this thing called the habit loop. It's basically a three-step neurological pattern that divides habits into different aspects. Understanding each of the aspects and the role they play in the habit formation process can help you recognize how negative habits are triggered, how you can avoid them, and how you can build positive ones instead. These aspects include cues, routines, and rewards. Now that you have an understanding let's look at these categories in more detail.

1. **Cue**

The cue is basically the first step in the habit loop. It's what tells your brain what you need to do. The cue acts as a trigger for a particular action or behavior. It is what sets you off. Most people think they know what triggers the bad habits. However, I've often found that not to be the case. You see, cues vary from person to person. What might be a cue for you might not even be worth noticing to someone else. That said, however, cues generally be a location, time, an emotional state of mind, or a preceding action.

2. **Routine**

The routine is basically the action or series of actions that are triggered by the cue. If you want to cultivate positive habits, the one thing that you need to know is that routine is the most crucial element that you need to focus on. This aspect of the habit loop is what you'll need to change to eliminate bad habits, and it's also the one you'll need to reinforce if you want to cultivate positive habits.

3. **Reward**

The reward is basically the desired result of performing an action. It's what helps you determine whether or not you should pursue an action triggered by the cue and if a particular habit loop is worth remembering. What you need to know about this aspect is that it basically provides you with positive reinforcement for your behavior. This reinforcement is what makes it more likely for you to repeat a particular behavior in the future.

Now that you have an understanding of the habit loop let's see how this process plays out in real life. Let's say that someone has a bad habit of using social media excessively. However, if they want to break free from bad habits, they'll need to identify the three aspects of that habit loop within the context of this behavior.

So, in this particular case, getting a notification from a social media app would serve as the cue. The desire to find out who liked or commented on their picture will serve as the reward. From this point onwards, the cue will trigger their routine of checking and surfing social media apps for hours on end.

When you try to avoid bad habits, you'll realize soon enough that you can't necessarily stop all the cues or triggers that you may face in life. But this isn't something that should stop you from cultivating positive habits instead of negative ones. Although you may not have control over the cues in your life, you do have control over another aspect of the habit loop, like the routine.

And that right there, my dear friend, is how you'll break free from the vicious cycle of negative habits. To eliminate negative habits and cultivate positive ones, you must learn to diagnose the habit by answering a series of questions. We'll talk more about this later in the chapter. For now, let's look at why habits are an important aspect of our pursuit of success.

THE IMPORTANCE OF HABITS

Are you aiming for success in your life?

All of us have aspirations and goals, whether they are related to academics, finances, health, or exercise. We already established that, in order to achieve what we desire, it is crucial to engage in actions that bring us closer to our goals. Over time, these actions become ingrained as habits. However, some of these habits can hinder our progress, while others can contribute positively to a fulfilling and admirable life.

The significant impact of habits on our lives and achievements is truly remarkable. Habits lay the groundwork for our routines, shape our behaviors and actions, and ultimately define who we are. They guide our decision-making process and play a crucial role in how we overcome challenges. By understanding and harnessing the power of habits, we can unlock growth, enhance productivity, and pave our way for long-term success.

Believe it or not, your habits are what will determine if you succeed in life. A lot of people don't really give this fact the acknowledgment it deserves. Think about it: habits have a role to play in all aspects of your life. Your health, career, relationships, and spirituality are all linked to your habits in one way or another.

The habits you have in one aspect of your life can even have a positive or negative impact on other aspects of your life. You might have great habits when it comes to punctuality and work ethic, but if your relationship habits are not as good, they'll begin to impact your performance soon enough. This right here is a very basic example, but I think that you're beginning to see the full picture, so let's look at how habits can shape our lives.

THE ROLE OF HABITS IN SHAPING OUR LIVES AND SUCCESS

Imagine waking up with a sense of dread about the day. Your morning routine feels disorganized as you quickly shower and hastily eat breakfast. Then, you pack your bags before rushing out the door.

As soon as you step into the office environment, you are bombarded with emails and requests that pull you in directions. This overwhelming feeling makes it difficult to focus on completing any task at hand.

After a day at work, when you finally arrive home, you may find yourself lacking the energy to do more. So you just quickly heat up a frozen dinner before collapsing on the couch. The dishes pile up in the sink. Your exercise equipment gathers dust. That book you've been meaning to read remains untouched for months. This disorganized chaos can leave you feeling exhausted and discouraged.

What if things could be different? What if each day could bring a revitalizing flow that aligns with your priorities? Wouldn't it be amazing to get up early in the morning, go for a jog, enjoy your breakfast out on the deck, and then head on to work with some calming blues or jazz during the commute?

When you get back from work, you will have the time to cook a meal, do the dishes, work out, make your bed, and go to sleep. Dear friend, I'm here to tell you that you can indeed achieve this lifestyle, but it will require some work on your end. The key to such a life lies in cultivating positive habits.

You see, habits are like threads intricately woven into the fabric of your life. As you consistently practice actions over time, they become deeply ingrained and shape your days, guiding your path. The right habits act as a compass needle pointing towards your goals and creating momentum where each small victory fuels the next.

When you incorporate positive habits into your life, you can see a huge difference in your productivity and overall well-being. If you keep practicing this on a regular basis, actions that once required you to make an effort become a part of your very nature. You'll be able to stay on top of your goals and achieve true fulfillment in life.

With a renewed sense of determination, you can direct your energy towards growth and accomplishments. When your habits align with your goals, progress happens naturally. Starting the day with meditation can bring tranquility and clarity to help set a tone for the rest of the day. Maintaining an exercise regimen boosts energy levels and gives you the momentum you need to tackle the tasks that lie ahead.

Taking some time for yourself in the evenings is important for rest and rejuvenation. When you combine eating habits with quality sleep, it gives your body that extra bit of energy and boost it needs. However, our habits also have an impact on aspects of our lives. Cultivating gratitude, optimism, and self-belief plays a role in shaping our well-being.

It lays the groundwork for realizing our potential. Engaging in daily writing fosters creativity and self-reflection. Building connections with others creates a sense of community. Positive habits empower us to overcome limitations and write the story of our lives. They help us break through the barriers that hold us back, allowing us to make progress one step at a time. It's like building blocks stacked upon each other. This momentum propels us forward and helps us achieve our goals.

With each habit we adopt, we lay down another stepping stone on the path toward becoming ourselves. We become who we aspire to be through the choices we make, and this comes together to form the tapestry of our lives. A true masterpiece, if you ask me.

STRATEGIES FOR BREAKING HABITS AND FORMING ONES

When we're cultivating positive habits, we need to have both patience and resilience. While it may be challenging, embarking on this journey can bring about rewards in terms of well-being and personal achievements.

Now, as promised, let's get back to the habit loop we talked about earlier in the chapter. Remember, we established that there are certain cues in life that trigger behaviors in pursuit of the desired result. To truly transform your life, you need to understand that these aspects can influence both your negative and positive habits.

In addition, you can use these aspects to eliminate negative habits and cultivate positive ones. The process may seem challenging at first, but trust me when I tell you that there's nothing in the world that can't be accomplished with some effort and commitment. Below, I've shared a few things you can do to overcome negative patterns and unlock your potential.

- The first thing you need to do is start by pinpointing the triggers that lead to these habits. Whether they arise from situations, emotions, or thought patterns, recognizing these cues allows you to anticipate them and address them mindfully. When you are able to spot that cue, you can keep it from triggering you to perform behaviors that are not beneficial.

- Once you've identified the triggers, it's time to replace them with alternatives. Instead of engaging in behaviors, try incorporating uplifting rituals into your daily life that energize and empower you. For instance, rather than snacking when bored or stressed, consider taking a walk. At this stage, all we're aiming to do is identify negative behaviors and replace them with positive ones. We can do this one habit at a time.

- Throughout this process, utilizing reminders, substitutions, and rewards can be highly beneficial. Place motivational quotes in spots as reminders of your goals. This will replace cues that take you off track with ones that keep you focused on your goals. Swap out negative behaviors for positive ones whenever possible. And don't forget to celebrate victories along the way. Remember, they serve as reinforcement and help maintain constructive habits.

- Visualization is another tool that can be helpful when adopting positive habits. Envision yourself embracing these habits in your life – imagine the confidence, vitality, and sense of accomplishment they will bring you. This mental imagery strengthens your dedication and motivation, helping you cultivate positive habits like never before.

- Another thing you can do to eliminate negative habits is to explore fulfilling hobbies. Pursuing hobbies gives us a sense of true fulfillment and keeps us from giving in to cues that trigger negative behavior. So basically, you should engage in activities that inspire growth while simultaneously steering you away from behaviors.

- Nurture relationships as vital support systems on your journey towards breaking free from old patterns. In situations where challenges become particularly overwhelming or complex to handle, it can be beneficial to seek assistance through support groups or counseling services. Having guidance during tough times offers different perspectives and much-needed support to understand the problem and make progress.

Lastly, it's important to remember that progress is not always a path that's easy to walk on; there may be setbacks along the way. However, by staying focused on long-term goals and acknowledging setbacks, you can stay on track toward achieving your desired outcomes. However, you must know that embarking on this path requires courage.

The positive habits you cultivate will pave the way for a life filled with passion and the realization of your potential.

And that, my dear friend, is how you cultivate positive habits in life. As you advance on your journey in pursuit of success, you will soon realize that the art of making progress is closely tied to effective planning, and we're not going to leave that stone unturned.

See you in the next chapter.

DEVELOPING EFFECTIVE TIME MANAGEMENT SKILLS

Understanding the importance of time is vital in life. There is no going around that. It allows us to gain experiences and develop skills as we navigate through our journey. But what exactly is time? Is that a matter of sheer precautions that some of the smartest scientists and philosophers continue to ponder upon? Is it the clock time and the hours and minutes going back? Or is it something else entirely?

When it comes to achieving success, time serves as the organizing force that encompasses the past and the future and has a sense of permanence. Each one of us has our own timeline on this planet, which becomes evident through how we change over the years. Just think about yourself a decade ago – your appearance and knowledge were undoubtedly different from what they are today. The world around us also evolves as time continues to progress.

Recognizing the value of time and its impact on success plays a role in maximizing productivity, achieving goals, and leading a fulfilling life. To understand the importance of time, you must see it as a resource that can truly transform your life. Use it wisely, and it can propel you to levels of unparalleled excellence. Ignore it, and it becomes your worst nightmare.

Over the years, I have seen many people waste quite a lot of time, and trust me when I tell you that time has a sneaky way of slipping away. You won't know that you're wasting it until it's too late. That's when you begin to see evident effects in your life, and trust me. These effects are anything but good.

Wasting time can have an influence on our success as it prevents us from achieving what we truly desire. When we fully grasp this concept, each day becomes an opportunity. Then, feeling lost or letting our goals fade away into obscurity is a concern that can hold us back. However, this is only possible when we acknowledge the fact that we're wasting time.

The thought of that novel, those unexplored business ideas, or neglected relationships weighs heavily on your mind. You realize that you have the potential to accomplish more but often find yourself battling against the inertia of procrastination. Have you ever thought about finding the motivation to truly make the most of every moment?

If you're someone who's actively pursuing success, you probably have. I'll let you in on a little secret: it all comes down to recognizing the power that lies within time passing by. To truly acknowledge the value of time being wasted, think about each second as a gold coin. Now imagine those coins slipping through your fingers one by one.

How would you handle that? Would you try to stop them slipping away? Would you spend each one intentionally? Or would you recklessly squander them on pointless pursuits? If you're committed to making it big in life, you'll probably keep the gold coins safe and use them on things that push in the right direction.

Time, dear friend, is no different. When we forget the worth of time, our priorities become blurred. Urgent tasks overshadow what truly matters, and distractions loom large while our dreams are put on hold. However, when we cherish every moment, our choices align accordingly.

By understanding the value of time, productivity thrives. You effortlessly transition from one task to another in a flow. Meaningful work is completed according to schedule, and proper planning helps us avoid stress and achieve our goals.

Valuing time also empowers us to set goals and pursue objectives. We develop plans to achieve them step by step. Procrastination and indecision diminish in the face of action, and consistent small victories propel us forward at pace. With each utilized hour, we derive satisfaction and find contentment when we strike a balance between work, relationships, and taking care of ourselves.

By acknowledging the value of time, we can make sure that it's not an element that governs our lives but an element we leverage to control and improve our lives. Now, some of us might think that they know how to manage time. But do they? I wouldn't be so sure. Acknowledging the importance of time and using it to our benefit goes way beyond creating a mere to-do list or a schedule. However, it's not something that can't be done.

So, with that in mind, let's look at some of the best ways you can manage your time more effectively.

STRATEGIES FOR PRIORITIZING TASKS AND EFFICIENT TIME MANAGEMENT

Before we get into how you can manage time more effectively, first, you need to think of it like art. It is an art you can craft using different tools and resources. The underlying fundamental behind effective time management is to see time as a resource that you budget and allocate. All of us have things in our lives that we must do and things that can be left unattended at the current moment.

We need to make note of what these things are and allocate the appropriate amount of time for each. However, this is something that's pretty easy to say. Why do I say that, you ask? Well, since we've already called time management an art, allow me to paint a picture. You might have decided to allocate time to your health.

For this purpose alone, you make a plan to work out every evening. The goal is to burn off the fat and build lean muscle. Now, you have allocated the appropriate amount of time for this goal, but think about what happens when an "urgent" deadline creeps up. You change your time budget and allocate the workout time to meet the office deadline.

You had found the time to work out, but as soon as life happened, effective time management became not so effective, didn't it? This is exactly why managing time without the necessary tools at your disposal becomes increasingly difficult. I've been there, and I understand how difficult it can get. That's exactly why I'll share some of the most valuable strategies that can help you make the most of your time. Let's look at what they are and divide deep into each one.

- The Eisenhower Matrix, also known as the Urgent Important Matrix, is a tool for categorizing tasks based on their importance and urgency. This approach basically consists of drawing a graph where the x-axis represents urgency and non-urgency, and the y-axis represents importance and non-importance. Using this approach, you have a total of four categories that you can allocate tasks and activities to. These categories include.

  - Urgent and Important.

  - Important but Not Urgent.

  - Urgent but Not Important.

  - Not Urgent and Not Important.

After labeling that graph using this format, you can add tasks and activities to each category. It's important for you to know that the tasks mentioned in the first category are those that should be performed immediately. Tasks that are listed in the second category are still important but not urgent, meaning that you can allocate time for them and perform them at a later date.

In the third category, you list tasks that are urgent but not important. These are the tasks you need to delegate. It's important to understand that such tasks may be urgent but are not important with regard to your pursuit of success and fulfillment and, therefore, don't require your involvement. In the last category, you list tasks that are neither urgent nor important.

It goes without saying that these are the tasks that you need to either postpone or eliminate since they don't require your immediate attention and can't propel you toward your goals. Now, let's move on to the next one.

- The ABCDE Method is basically a priority-setting technique that was invented by Brian Tracy. The best thing about this method is that it is pretty simple to use. All you have to do is prioritize your tasks and activities using the first five letters of the alphabet. Each letter helps you assign a level of priority to different tasks and activities as follows.

  - A - Most Important

  - B - Second Most Important

  - C - Non-urgent task

  - D - Tasks that can be delegated

  - E - Tasks that should be eliminated

I'm pretty sure that you don't really need an explanation on how to prioritize tasks using this method and I won't go into those details. However, I will share some valuable tips that will come in handy when you use this method. So, let's begin. When it comes to using the ABCDE method, the first thing that you must do is make time for the 'A' tasks.

Remember, these are the ones that are most important, and you should commit to only one at a time. Another thing you need to do when working on 'A' tasks is to get rid of all the distractions beforehand. Think back to the cues we talked about in the last chapter. They're what you'll want to avoid here.

Another thing you do to make this method more effective is to determine a time frame for your ABCDE list. Think about it: Do you want the list to determine weekly, bi-weekly, or monthly tasks and then write them down? Another thing you should always keep in mind is that you should never work on a task that's not on the list. Now, let's move on to the next one.

1. The Pareto Principle, also referred to as the "80/20 Rule," suggests that 80% of results stem from 20% of efforts. Given this, it can be stated that to optimize your results, it is crucial to identify and prioritize the tasks that will generate outcomes and allocate all efforts appropriately.

    Most people often confuse this rule when it comes to applying it to time management. To manage time using this rule, you must understand that a mere 20% of your time, if allocated appropriately, will lead to 80% of your results. However, before you do that, you must assess your own capabilities and level of performance.

    After you've done that, you'll need to separate unimportant tasks from important ones. However, the criteria for this separation will be based on your understanding of which task you believe will lead to 80% of the desired results with 20% of the efforts. Being able to use this method effectively will allow you to get better results with more manageable efforts.

There are a lot of other time management methods out there that you can use to allocate this valuable resource more effectively. However, I won't go into all the details here because the underlying principle of all these methods is that you must organize tasks based on urgency and importance. So, let's take a brief look at what some of these methods are.

One of these methods is time blocking. Now, this method is a bit different than the others in terms of approach. It basically states that instead of dividing by the amount required to complete certain tasks, you need to divide your days into blocks. Once you do that, you need to group together tasks based on their similarities.

Then, you dedicate each block of the day to a specific task or a group of tasks. So, if you've divided your day into three blocks, one for professional work, one for your personal chores, and the other for spirituality, in each of these time slots, you'll only perform tasks for that particular category.

The next one on the list is the Pomodoro Technique. This technique basically revolves around allocating your time to different tasks based on 25-minute intervals known as Pomodoros. So basically, you work on your first task for a Pomodoro and then take a 5-minute break. After the break, you continue working on the task until you've made the desired amount of progress.

It goes without saying that tasks in this method are also prioritized based on urgency and importance. Once you've completed four Pomodoro's, you can take a slightly longer break. The method empowers you to achieve your goals by allowing you to work in intervals. This gives you a chance to take a break here and there, build up your energy, and complete tasks without experiencing complete burnout.

The last method for time management that I'd find to be very, and I mean very, effective is something called "Eat That Frog." I'll start with a brief origin story before going into the details of what this method really is all about. Mark Twain, one of the best publishers and writers in American history, once said, "If it's your job to eat a frog, it's best to do it first thing in the morning. And If it's your job to eat two frogs, it's best to eat the biggest one first."

Now, he wasn't really talking about exotic dishes here. The word "Frog" in this context refers to a difficult task. It's that one task all of us have been holding back and don't feel too confident about. Now, it's important to understand that when we hold back on an important task, we continue to think (some might worry) about it subconsciously.

This right here keeps you focusing and performing well on the tasks that you're currently performing. Now, what Brian Tracy did is he took this particular quote and turned it into a time management method. So, when you're using the "Eat Your Frog" method to manage your time, you'll basically do the most difficult task first thing in the morning.

This way, you have the rest of the day to work on all your other tasks with greater focus, as you won't have anything hanging over your head. Remember that everyone has requirements when it comes to task completion and time management. It's essential to explore approaches to determine what works best for you.

With practice and self-discipline, you can enhance productivity and make better use of your time. Now, dear reader, I would urge you to try these methods and figure out which one would be best for you. Then, in the next chapter, we'll focus on how you can build a supportive network and enhance your relationship.

CHAPTER 8

BUILDING A SUPPORTIVE NETWORK

Before we start this chapter, I want you to know that having a support system in life is very, very important. When most people hear the word "support system" or "support network," they often believe this is something that is for those who are weak. However, that is not true, and you need to break free from such beliefs if you want to actually comprehend the value of having a support system.

It changes your perspective on success and helps you understand the steps needed to achieve your goals. Throughout the journey of life, all of us encounter several trials, face many defeats, and overcome countless challenges. Life, indeed, is filled with tons of uncertainties and a load of vulnerabilities.

It is important to acknowledge the fact that some of these experiences can be overwhelming when faced alone. This is why having a support system becomes incredibly valuable. Whether it includes family members, friends, colleagues, or mentors, a strong support system provides assistance and practical help when needed most.

Recognizing and nurturing such a network significantly impacts our well-being, personal growth, and overall success. You see, in life, there arc always people who are just trying to bring us down. The worst of it is that most people don't even realize who these people are. They are our foes, but they also are our "friends."

However, developing a support system means you free yourself from such toxicity in life. In a support network, all the people you are are like-minded individuals who believe in personal and professional development, uplifting others and are on their own pursuit of success. These are people who firmly believe that they can not get ahead by pulling others back.

These people believe in providing necessary support and guidance to each other. They foster a better environment for all the members of that group. This helps them gain a new perspective on life and opens their mindset to previously undiscovered possibilities. Believe it or not, these are some rare qualities to have in people, especially today.

When building a support network, you must always remember that these are the type of people you want to have. We'll go into more detail about this throughout this chapter. For now, let's look at the importance of having a support group.

THE IMPORTANCE OF HAVING A SUPPORT SYSTEM

Have you ever felt the desire to connect with others and share your thoughts and emotions? As human beings, it's only natural for us to seek companionship. However, in our pursuit of success, we must ensure that such companionship is one that fosters both growth and productivity.

It's important to understand that both these outcomes can only come from having a competent support network. Being a part of like-minded individuals can affect our own perception and help us tackle all the curveballs life throws at us. But that's not all. Since people in our support network are likely to have similar challenges and pursuits as we do, engaging with them can help us share positive feedback as well.

As someone who's looking to achieve success in all aspects of life, you must understand that having a network of support is crucial because it allows us to freely express ourselves, let go of our worries, and find comfort during times. When we have people who genuinely listen and understand us, it validates our emotions. This validation not only helps reduce stress but also contributes to our overall mental well-being.

Have you ever experienced challenges in life where you thought that you were the only one who felt this way? Chances are you probably have (I know I certainly did). Now, it's important to understand these feelings can negatively impact our mental health. Thinking that we're the only ones who feel a certain way can lead to self-isolation and a lack of meaning in life.

When we're part of a support network where others truly understand how we feel, we can open up about the challenges or problems we face. This allows us to gain and give valuable feedback that reduces stress, improves our mental health, and empowers us with solutions we can actually implement in our life to achieve the results we desire.

As humans, we are inherently creatures who crave connection and communication with others. Establishing a support system means having individuals with whom we can share both the happy and sad moments of life. Our successes and failures alike. This emotional support serves as a foundation in our lives.

This is indeed what allows us to believe that we're not the only ones who need to feel the way we do. It gives us the much-needed support to get through difficult times and tackle challenges head-on. In addition, it allows us to share our wins in life, be appreciated for them, and know that when we share our accomplishments, we are also encouraging others to do better in life.

Life often presents us with obstacles. From struggles to setbacks in our lives. In these situations, having a support system becomes invaluable as it provides guidance, advice, and fresh perspectives. Whether we are faced with decisions or dealing with the aftermath of failure, having someone reliable to lean on can greatly shape how we navigate through these tests.

You see, sometimes in life, we're just too close to a problem to see what's actually going on. Our ability to fully comprehend the challenge becomes a bit cloudy and impacts our decision-making. However, sharing the problem or challenge with people in our support network helps us gain multiple perspectives we can use to come up with a solution and continue our pursuit of success.

Building resilience requires having a network of people around us; therefore, having a support system is essential. Knowing that there are individuals who believe in us and are willing to offer assistance can significantly boost our self-confidence. It's important to cultivate this mindset when faced with circumstances.

It reminds us that we are not alone in our challenges and that there are resources to help us. When we strive towards our goals, having a support system can make a big difference. Whether we're seeking job opportunities, embarking

on journeys, or pursuing our dreams, surrounding ourselves with inspiring individuals who provide feedback and
motivation is truly invaluable.

They offer insights based on their experiences and empower us to surpass the limits we perceive. We can learn from
their expertise and develop solutions based on the stories
they have to tell. But that is not all. We can also share our
own experiences with them, allowing others to learn from
what we've gone through and how we dealt with it.

Research consistently shows the impact of having a network of support on both our physical well-being. Numerous studies emphasize the connection between having a
circle of support and overall improved health. When we
have someone to share our joys with, it amplifies our happiness; similarly, confiding in others during difficult times
helps alleviate stress and reduce anxiety levels.

Additionally, being part of a community can expedite re-
covery from illnesses or setbacks as their presence and
care contribute to our well-being. The sense of belonging
is crucial for our fulfillment. It provides us with a sense of
connection to others, fulfilling a need in our lives. Having
people who support us grants acceptance and a feeling of
belongingness where we can freely be ourselves without
fearing judgment.

Now that you know the importance of support groups,
we need to understand that support groups or networks
primarily work on the relationships we build and nurture
with. Let's look at how we can do just that.

TIPS FOR BUILDING AND NURTURING RELATIONSHIPS

In order to succeed in both our professional and personal lives, the strength of our relationships is incredibly important. Meaningful connections enable collaboration, support, and opportunities for growth. Whether it's within our work circles or in our community, cultivating and nurturing relationships requires effort and genuine care for others. So, with that in mind, let's explore some strategies to foster these relationships:

- **Communication**

  Successful relationships thrive on honest communication. It's crucial to be a listener and consider other people's perspectives. Engaging in conversations where you express your thoughts while remaining receptive to their feedback helps build trust and understanding, both of which are the foundation for partnerships.

  However, remaining receptive is not something that most people can do. It takes time. To do this, you need to be an active listener. You need to listen to their problems and truly understand them. When you do, people will see that you value what they have, and this right is what will help develop trust.

- **Empathy and Understanding**

  Demonstrating empathy creates an environment that fosters care, compassion, appreciation, and respect for those you interact with. Acknowledging their emotions and experiences helps cultivate connections while building esteem. But, to do this, you must be able to "walk a mile in their shoes."

This means that you need to see the world like they do. You must understand their challenges as they are yours now. You need to feel what they are, even if it's for a brief moment. This will help you better comprehend where the other person is coming from and will give you feedback others can actually apply.

- **Reliability and Trustworthiness**

Consistently demonstrating dependability through both actions and commitments is key to forming connections with others. People naturally gravitate towards those they can rely on over time. It is important to avoid making promises you cannot keep and ensure that you follow through on what you say.

Those who are in need of some help love to see a hand reaching out to them. However, if that hand is yours, it doesn't give false hope. Telling someone who trusts you that you'll do something for them and not following through with it will destroy your trustworthiness. More importantly, it can damage the other person to an extent where they may be able to trust anyone ever again.

- **Supportive Encouragement**

Being there for people during both their successes and struggles is essential in building relationships. Offer help, guidance, and motivation whenever they need it. Celebrate their achievements with them and uplift them as they experience situations that may challenge their abilities.

Doing this will help foster a relationship where both partners feel as if they are not alone in the world. Trust me when I say that this feeling, sometimes in life, is the best thing someone experiences. It might be the one that gives them the added boost and momentum needed to carry on in the right direction.

- **Respect and Care**

It is crucial to treat everyone with respect and care regardless of their identity or occupation. Such behavior creates a culture that values different perspectives and experiences. The world is filled with people who come from different cultures and backgrounds.

People have varying experiences and are exposed to different circumstances and occupational opportunities in life. However, it's important to understand that such differences don't, and should never, govern the respect or care we give to others. To foster valuable relations, you must learn to respect people for what they are, not what they do or what they've been through.

- **Be Genuine and Authentic**

Stay true to yourself and sincerely engage in your relationships. People appreciate honesty and are more likely to trust and connect with those who are genuine. Avoid pretending to be someone you're not, as authenticity is key for building lasting connections.

However, you must understand what others face, believe, and want to become might differ from you entirely. This doesn't mean that your relationship with them won't be effective. In fact, the truth about effective relationships doesn't lie in having similarities. It lies within accepting differences.

- **Collaborate and Share**

Another thing you can do to build a truly competent support network is to actively seek opportunities to work together and exchange information in both your personal and professional relationships. This helps show your partner that you care for them and are willing to help them achieve their goals.

However, to do this, you must first believe that their goals, objectives, and ambitions are yours as well. Once you develop this belief, you begin to dedicate yourself to your partner as if you are doing it for your own self. This helps develop trust, improves collaboration, and allows you to develop lasting relations.

Building relationships and personal growth can be achieved by embracing collaboration and sharing ideas. Collaborating with others does not foster creativity. Also expands networks, leading to valuable outcomes.

It's important to be mindful of boundaries when forming connections. Understanding and respecting limits is essential, as well as considering the privacy of others. Being attentive to their comfort levels while balancing support with giving space is the key to nurturing bonds. Remember that you don't want to come off as too strong.

Another great thing you can do is to appreciate the efforts other people make for you. Showing gratitude, whether through a "thank you" or a heartfelt gesture, strengthens relationships. Encourages support from those around you. Being a trustworthy person can have an impact on the others in your life. Therefore, you need to spread positive energy and motivate and inspire the people in your circle. Believe it or not, optimism and excitement are contagious. However, to leverage, you must have the power to bring happiness wherever you go.

Attending networking events and conferences related to your field gives you the opportunity to connect with individuals, both familiar faces and new acquaintances. Engaging in these events allows you to nurture existing connections while also forging ones. It's important to understand that these connections serve as a valuable resource that you can give to your support group.

They help you gain a new perspective on your professional life. Using technology such as media platforms and business networking tools can effectively help you connect with your contacts. However, it's important to remember that in-person interactions often carry more influence than online relationships. The last component to building an effective support network is finding a mentor or role model. Let's look at that in more detail.

SEEKING MENTORS AND ROLE MODELS

When it comes to seeking mentors and role models, I cannot emphasize enough how game-changing this strategy can be. These individuals become a source of guidance, encouragement, and insight as you navigate situations on your path toward success. Mentors and role models possess the knowledge, experience, and admirable qualities that you aspire to acquire.

By emulating their characteristics, you can make an impact on your own growth journey. There are many reasons why seeking out mentors and role models is essential. In this discussion, we will delve into their importance further while providing some guidance along the way. You must understand that seeking out a mentor can help you in a number of ways.

For example, drawing from their experiences can help you learn and propel your personal and professional growth. Having mentors and role models who have already walked the path you aspire to tread can provide guidance. By observing their successes and setbacks, you can accelerate your development while avoiding obstacles by anticipating them ahead of time.

The insights offered by a mentor can be transformative, propelling your growth in aspects of many different aspects of life. Having the right mentor can help you excel in personal aspects of life, such as your relationship. In addition, learning from one can also help you get the skills you need to excel in your career.

Their perspectives shed light on the way you are likely to walk. They can help you set realistic goals for yourself. Therefore, you need to embrace their wisdom as you navigate your journey toward success. When someone you admire believes in you and offers words of encouragement, it can greatly impact how you perceive yourself.

Seeing the achievements and resilience of your role models will inspire confidence in your abilities and will motivate you to strive for greater accomplishments. Trust me when I tell you that the "If they can do it, so can I" mindset really makes a difference in life. It helps you eliminate self-doubt, instills confidence, and propels you in the right direction.

Connecting with mentors and role models opens doors to opportunities. They can introduce you to individuals who may become connections in your professional network. Building relationships with people expands your chances for collaborations and potential growth. But it doesn't end there. This can also help you build and foster an effective support network.

A mentor's guidance is instrumental in developing skills that lead to success. Their constructive criticism helps improve communication, leadership, and decision-making abilities, allowing your talent to be honed effectively. Most people often face challenges when faced with a decision pertaining to the navigation of their professional lives and which career options to pursue.

When faced with a decision on which path to pursue, seeking guidance from a mentor can provide clarity. They can assist you in understanding how to leverage your interests and abilities in the world. This can help you be more focused and accountable in the world. The presence of a mentor by your side is truly invaluable.

They help keep you focused and ensure that you take ownership of your actions. Regular check-ins and receiving feedback are crucial in order to avoid distractions and stay motivated. However, finding someone who is right for you as a mentor can be a bit challenging.

HOW TO FIND A MENTOR

When you are looking to find a mentor, it's important not to overlook the people you already have in your circle. Your colleagues, friends, or family members may possess the wisdom and support you're looking for. Additionally, don't underestimate the mentors within your community. Stepping out of your comfort zone allows you to connect with mentors at conferences and events where esteemed professionals gather.

Expressing admiration for their work while asking questions can lay the foundation for growth. As I've said earlier, finding a mentor that's right for you can be challenging. However, this doesn't mean that it's something that can be done. Two ways that have helped me find mentors that were right for me include:

- **Utilizing Platforms for Direct Outreach**

To find the right mentor, you can take advantage of platforms like LinkedIn to reach out directly to experts whose work inspires you. When reaching out to them, you need to share how their experiences and knowledge could contribute to shaping your success story.

You must remember to be bold in seeking guidance from individuals whom you deeply respect. You can also pursue exploring associations and alumni groups, which often present mentoring opportunities that offer perspectives and advice from those who have walked in your shoes.

If online mentorship is convenient for you, consider exploring platforms that connect mentors with mentees who are seeking growth opportunities. These digital tools, on a scale, greatly expand your options and possibilities. However, if you prefer a more one approach to mentorship, there is something else you can try.

- **Nonprofit organizations**

These organizations can also serve as valuable resources for individuals seeking to achieve personal and professional development goals through mentorship. One thing you must remember is in such organizations, volunteer work opens doors to mentor relationships.

When reaching out to mentors, it's important to acknowledge and respect the value of their time. You can do this by showing curiosity about their background. Try asking them what their source of motivation was. You must listen attentively to their answers and seek applicable insights from their experience.

It's important to understand that you need to have an effective relationship with your mentor and that such relationships are only formed when you truly comprehend and admire your mentor's work. When it comes to receiving guidance from them, you must always remain open-minded.

Working with prejudice is not going to be helpful here. Accept the knowledge and insight that come from their mentorship programs and the casual encounter you have with them. Most people often overlook casual encounters, but you need to know that wisdom can often come from such interactions.

Lastly, the underlying principle here from building a support network and finding a mentor is to not be stringent with what you already believe. The key here is to understand that you may not know everything and that it's absolutely okay. You need to welcome all new experiences, advice, and guidance that a support network or a mentor has to offer.

In addition, you must also make sure that this is the environment you foster when building your own support group. And that, dear friend, is how you can develop a support network that's truly dedicated to providing help and uplifting others. In the next chapter, we'll talk about an aspect of life that many deem to be too important and one that's a goal for all of us: money.

FINANCIAL SUCCESS AND WEALTH CREATION

After reading the title of the chapter, you might experience something that's similar to cognitive dissonance. Right now, you're probably thinking that at the beginning of the book, we stated being successful in life has nothing to do with the money you have or earn. Remember that? Well, if that's the case, why are we discussing that now?

Allow me to explain. You see, success is never about money. However, money is a significant part of success, just like personal and professional growth, spirituality, and all the other things we've discussed in the book so far. Before we dive into this chapter, I want you to know that people give varying importance to each aspect of success.

For some, money is the most important one, but for others, personal development and spirituality might be the top two. Now, what you need to understand here is that everyone is free to make their own choices and have their own priorities. Remember what we learned in the first chapter?

All of us interpret success differently than others. However, the end definition still revolves around the aspect we've discussed in the book. Money, like all others, is one of these aspects. Why, you ask? Well, that's because the underlying principle of the pursuit of success is to achieve prosperity, and this is something that you can not do with achieving financial excellence.

However, to achieve financial success, you must learn to diversify your income, increase your savings and investment, and budget towards your goals and ambitions. We'll cover all of these things in this chapter. However, before we do that, let's ponder upon why financial success is important first.

THE IMPORTANCE OF FINANCIAL SUCCESS

Well, the reason lies in the fact that financial success is closely tied to having the resources you need to do whatever it is you really want to do. Think about it: you want a roof for your family, and you need money. You want your kids to have what you never did. You need money. If you want to help those less fortunate, you need money.

Without the money, it becomes challenging to achieve well-being, as we've defined in this book. While money alone doesn't solely determine success, it does have an impact on our well-being, opportunities, and ability to accomplish our goals and dreams. It's important to remember that financial success is one aspect of defining success.

Despite this, you must never forget that its significance should be balanced with factors that contribute to a fulfilling life. These factors encompass growth, meaningful relationships, happiness, and a sense of purpose. All these elements contribute to success, and all of them require equal acknowledgment and effort.

Would you want to have all the money in the world without having any meaningful relationships, personal development, or advancement opportunities in life? Would you rather be rich and not connected to your inner self and live a life without purpose? You wouldn't, would you? Therefore, you need to understand the role money has to play.

UNDERSTANDING THE ROLE OF FINANCIAL SUCCESS

Understanding the role of money can evoke countless emotions. Some perceive money as a corrupting influence or as the root of greed and evil. Others view it as a facilitator of dreams. To understand the role money has to play in our lives, we must first abandon the belief that money is either good or bad.

The truth, dear friend, is that money is neither good nor bad on its own. Money simply amplifies the attitudes and beliefs one already has and allows them to express what they want in a tangible form. Imagine a person who admires material possessions but the monetary resources to own them.

What do you think they'll do when they get money? On the other hand, imagine a person who wants to support their family and those in need but they don't currently possess the monetary resources to do so. What do they think they'll do when they first get the money? I think this little example is enough for you to comprehend that money is just an amplified expression of what already exists.

Achieving financial success can unlock both positive and negative opportunities in life. This right here is why money shouldn't be the most important aspect of your success. You must first discover who you are and what your purpose is. This way, when you do achieve financial success, your monetary behaviors will be aligned with who you really are.

Just imagine experiencing freedom from constraints and being able to invest in yourself and your highest aspirations. Opportunities come knocking, offering you access to education, professional networks, and the tools you need for personal growth. Your distant dreams are now starting to come into focus.

Attaining freedom acts as a springboard for self-actualization. When your needs are no longer a struggle, you have more energy to pursue goals like learning, creating, and making contributions to causes that extend beyond yourself. However, it's important to remember that money alone cannot guarantee fulfillment.

True success involves finding a balance between stability and other aspects of life, such as health, relationships, and purpose. Nevertheless, by reducing worries, you can establish a foundation that removes obstacles on your journey towards living your life. Financial achievement also allows you to uplift others.

You can support your family, contribute to causes, and pass on prosperity for generations. Keep in mind that true wealth is not measured by what you accumulate but rather by what you share with others. However, you must remember that money should never define who you are as an individual.

When used wisely and responsibly, it has the potential to empower your ambitions. Financial success helps remove any limitations holding you back so that you can carve a path towards becoming the version of yourself while making a lasting impact. Remember, every journey begins with taking that step.

So, with that in mind, let's look at how you can build a solid foundation for financial success.

BUILDING THE FOUNDATION OF FINANCIAL SUCCESS

Building a foundation and effectively managing personal finances are crucial steps toward achieving stability and reaching your aspirations. Many individuals often face challenges when it comes to handling their finances. Moving forward requires developing disciplined habits and having foresight.

However, this is something that is easy to say but actually quite challenging to do. Most people in life have something that's casually referred to as "My money keeps vanishing into thin air." Based on my experiences, I've found that these people are completely unaware of how they spend their money and tend to live a paycheck lifestyle.

You might be unfamiliar with what that term really means. The paycheck lifestyle is when you only have enough money to cover monthly needs and expenses, and in some cases, even that becomes challenging. People who live the paycheck lifestyle are left with little to no spending potential at the end of each month until they get their salary.

However, this scenario can be avoided by developing solid financial foundations. This is something that I've challenged head-on in life, and I've come up with some practical tips that can help you do the same. These tips include:

- Begin by creating a budget that outlines all your sources of income and expenses. This will provide you with an understanding of how your money flows in and out of your life, helping you identify areas where improvements can be made.

  By being mindful of your expenses and finding ways to reduce costs, you can embrace the virtue of frugality. This means you'll be able to cut down on unnecessary expenses and have some extra cash left over for a rainy day.

- Treat investing as a ritual in your life. Set aside a portion of your income on a basis to contribute towards savings accounts and emergency funds. Allow time and the power of compounding to work in your favor by exploring investment options.

  However, you must remember that it's essential to keep your investment portfolio diversified. This means that you need to have an ideal mix of stocks, bonds, and assets that increase in monetary value.

- Define goals for yourself, whether it's starting a business, purchasing a home, or funding education. Having planned objectives gives you direction and motivation to stay on track. Break down these goals into milestones to make them more achievable.

You can divide your financial goals into three categories: short-term, mid-term, and long-term. Short-term goals that you can achieve with monetary savings of around one year or slightly longer.

Mid-term goals, on the other hand, may require you to save and invest for a period of anywhere between three to five years. Whereas long-term goals cannot be achieved with savings alone, rely on investment returns, and may take longer than five years.

- Live within your means by resisting the temptation of debt through spending that aligns with your needs and priorities. Most people often feel pressured by milestones society has imposed on them and tend to fall into the debt trap to achieve them.

Or just tend to spend more than they make. However, to have a solid financial foundation, you need to make sure that you only spend on what's necessary and avoid things that serve as an expression of your impulsive desires.

It's important to understand the difference between necessary purchases and purposeful ones. Achieving freedom relies on maintaining a balance between your income and expenses.

- To do this, you must categorize what you want to purchase based on "needs" and "wants." Purchases that fall in your "needs" category are those that are essential for survival.

However, you must understand that purchases that fall in your "wants" category are ones that aren't necessary for your survival. These are things that are just nice to have in life.

- To protect yourself from life's challenges, it's crucial to have insurance coverage for health, life, and property. Adequate insurance safeguards your assets and keeps you from experiencing financial disaster.

  Think about it for a second. If you're the only breadwinner in the house, what would happen to your family if you all of a sudden lost your job, experienced a disability, were caught up in a natural disaster, or any other uncertainty?

  That's where insurance coverage comes in. Having insurance allows you to ensure that if you ever experience an event that triggers monetary uncertainty, you have access to feasible funds to make it through.

- Make a commitment to enhancing your literacy by reading books, taking courses, and seeking advice from experts in the field. I cannot stress this enough, but this here is possibly one of the most important factors that contributes to your financial success.

  Having knowledge about finance is crucial when it comes to navigating your journey. It might be worth considering seeking guidance from an advisor who can provide assistance.

But not all you can do. As mentioned, there are a ton of different resources that you can learn from, and there are a ton of different things that you can learn. You gain knowledge about setting financial goals.

You can learn about creating a budget. You can become an expert in identifying and eliminating impulsive desires that trigger unnecessary spending. Then, you can use all this knowledge to allocate monetary resources to things that actually matter.

- Develop a habit of reviewing your budgets, goals, and strategies as life evolves. Adjustments may be necessary to align with the realities you face. It's important to acknowledge the fact that your monetary requirements will change as you progress through life.

What's important to you now might not hold value in the future, and things you haven't even thought about become paramount. This is exactly why you need to review your life and goals from time to time.

Once you've done that, you can use the insights derived from the review and compare them with your spending, saving, and investing budget. Remember that, in some cases, both these things might not align perfectly with each other, and that's okay.

However, you do need to make a dedicated and comprehensive effort to make sure that you change your budget based on where you're currently at in life and where it is you want to be.

Consistency, patience, and discipline are factors that contribute to financial success, and these are things you must strive to maintain while implementing the tips I've mentioned above. In addition, you must never compare yourself to others. The hard truth about life is that there will always be people who are ahead of you or have more money than you do.

However, this doesn't mean that those people are the competition. In fact, this doesn't even mean that competition exists. Think about it: if you have to take care of yourself, your family, and those you care about and pursue your ambition, do you really need to compete with the others? The plain and simple answer is "No!"

That's because no two people in the world are in the same race. Each one of us is running our own marathon. You must also understand that building a solid financial foundation won't happen overnight. It takes time, dedication, commitment, and effort. However, the results are worth it as they provide you with financial security and stability and allow you to explore countless opportunities.

When you've built a solid financial foundation, your journey to monetary success will be much easier. You'll have the resources to do what you want when you want. However, a solid foundation is only the first half of financial success. The other half is all about creating wealth. Let's look at what that's all about.

STRATEGIES FOR WEALTH CREATION

Before we get into the strategies that we can use to create wealth, let's look at what wealth really means. You see, wealth is about having abundant financial assets or assets that can be converted into monetary resources than what was initially paid for the assets.

The objective of wealth creation, as explained by Warren Buffet, is to find ways to generate income even while you sleep so you can escape the necessity of working until your death. This involves investing your existing funds to create a stream of income over time, which allows your savings to grow and enhance your earnings potential. Growing your wealth includes achieving both short-term and long-term goals. Short-term goals may involve saving for a vacation or buying an iPhone within three years or less. These goals often require investments or savings when compared to buying a car or making mortgage payments toward owning a house.

On the other hand, long-term goals like securing funds for retirement require time spanning several years or even decades. In such cases, it is crucial to ensure that the income earned during your working years is sufficient to meet your needs once you retire. To achieve our goals, it is crucial to consider the range of objectives and their respective timelines. Therefore, implementing strategies becomes vital in accomplishing these goals.

When it comes to exploring wealth creation strategies and investment options, many people lack the proper understanding. To achieve prosperity, it's important to approach investing while keeping your goals and values in mind. The key lies in exploring investment options and vehicles that allow you to prudently put your savings into action.

Creating wealth involves more than earning money. It also means investing a portion of your income to generate returns that grow over time. By using your saved funds, you can expand your assets and create an additional source of income for greater financial security. It's all about making the money do the hard work for you.

One key factor in maximizing returns is allowing the power of compound interest to work its magic over time. Starting early gives your money decades to grow and multiply. Remember, patience and consistency are crucial. Therefore, you need to avoid making decisions based on short-term market fluctuations.

It's important to understand that such changes often come as an immediate result of varying factors that may include news, politics, disasters, and other unpredictable events. However, immediate price fluctuations that come as a result of this event are often short-lived. Therefore, changing your investment strategy based on these factors is not something that I would recommend.

Instead, it is better to invest in vehicles that are less prone to market vulnerabilities and offer sustainable returns for a long period of time. As you progress in your career and gain experience, consider increasing the amount you contribute towards investments as your income grows. Aim to save a percentage for any salary raises you receive.

It's important to prioritize disciplined investing rather than chasing wins or getting involved in risky schemes. Remember, it's not about speed but about making progress. To manage risk and maximize rewards, it's essential to diversify your investment portfolio. Consider a mix of assets such as stocks, mutual funds, real estate, and fixed deposits based on your risk tolerance and stage of life.

Seeking trusted advice when needed can help you develop an investment strategy that is suited to specific needs and requirements. You must understand that true wealth is when you've removed monetary restrictions that keep you or the ones you love from doing what they want. Did you experience a childhood where you wanted something, but your parents weren't able to afford it?

Or do you know someone who did? Recall those memories or imagine what that would have felt like. Do you want our children to experience the same things? Chances are you probably don't. Now, imagine your children's laughter as they learn and grow without any limitations! That right there is what true wealth is all about.

This is something that all of us want to achieve in life, but the sad reality is very few of us make it to this point. The question you should ask yourself now is, "How can I bridge the gap between this vision and reality?" The answer to this question, dear friend, lies within building a solid financial foundation, savings, and investing.

Think of each financial opportunity as a piece of a puzzle that comes together to form a picture. It's the picture of your ideal life where you or your loved ones don't have to give up on their ambitions due to monetary restrictions. It's the picture of you owning your own house without any mortgage.

It's the picture where you help out somebody by giving them money for education so they can create a better life for themselves. It's the picture of you not holding back on your children's desires because your paycheck ran out. But, to turn this picture into a reality filled with happiness, joy, and gratitude, you need to focus on building wealth.

Now that you have an understanding of what a solid financial foundation is and why building wealth is important, let's look at some strategies that you can use to succeed in this pursuit.

- When investing, you must realize that stocks have the potential for returns but also come with volatility. It is advisable to conduct thorough research and hold them for the long term.

  When you invest in stocks, always remember not to put all your eggs in one basket. This means that you must diversify your stock portfolio. This way, if one of your investments plummets, you still can generate returns from others.

- Mutual funds provide a way to diversify your investments by pooling money from investors into assets. Index funds, in particular, remove the uncertainty of selecting stocks and offer exposure to the overall market.

Bonds are also a great way to rest assured that your initial capital is secure and that you are generating a return on it. All these are different investment options that are available for your exposure.

- If you are seeking income, without risk compared to stocks and bonds, fixed-income investments are options. They generate interest earnings over time. Real estate is another avenue that can provide income while also appreciating in value.

  You can choose to invest in properties or explore real estate investment trusts (REITs) for exposure. Based on my experience, I've always found real estate to be the safest investment option of all.

- If you're willing to take on some risk, startup or venture capital investments can provide the opportunity to own shares in companies that have the potential for growth. This can be quite an interesting and valuable pursuit.

  Think about it: you might not have had money to start your own business at an earlier point in time. However, investing in a startup allows you to experience what life has to offer down that avenue as well.

- Retirement accounts like 401(k)s allow for tax-deferred savings growth, which can be further boosted through employer matching contributions. Additionally, high-interest savings accounts allow your earnings to securely accumulate for short-term goals.

- Cryptocurrencies offer exposure to emerging assets such as Bitcoin and Ethereum. Although they are subject to volatility, there is also a potential for gains if you're daring enough.

- Annuities can also be worth considering since they offer guaranteed lifetime payouts that supplement retirement income. However, it's essential that you do your due diligence prior to pursuing this investment option.

It's crucial to work with a trusted advisor who can customize your investment portfolio based on your risk tolerance, goals, and time horizon. They will assist you in making decisions while steering clear of risks. Remember to maintain patience and consistency and stay well-informed throughout the process.

By diversifying your investments across vehicles and allowing your savings to grow over time, you will gradually establish a financial foundation that will protect you in the long term. Your money has the potential to help you turn yours into a reality. But first, you must learn to manage it effectively.

If I were to tell you how to do that in a quick minute, I would start by identifying how you spend your money and write down all the details. Once you've done that, you can then move on to analyzing each of your spending based on needs and wants. Remember, we talked about this earlier in the chapter.

Now, you need to calculate your total income. This includes your salary, bonuses, overtime pay, and the money you make from a part-time job, side hustle, or even the occasional garage sale. Once you have this information handy, you need to divide your income into three categories: expense, savings, and investing.

How much money you allocate to each category depends on your individual circumstances and is subject to change from time to time. However, a general rule that I personally like to follow is 40% of the income for expenses, 30% for savings, and 30% for investments. But we're not done just yet.

After creating a budget, as mentioned above, you need to divide the money you set aside for saving and investment even further. Now, there's no hard and fast rule about this, but when saving, you must first remember to create an emergency fund that accounts for at least 6 months of expenses if you have no income.

The emergency fund should be a top priority. Once you manage to do that, you can then begin to save for your short-, mid-, and long-term goals. Remember that one of these goals must be to have a substantial amount of monetary resources to acquire sustainable investment options. This is how you get the money to do the work for you and can ensure that you have diversified your income.

Now, it's important to understand that this, along with everything else in life, comes with different obstacles and challenges. We'll talk about this in the next chapter. For now, I want you to take what you've learned in the chapter and use it to build a solid financial foundation that'll propel you in the right direction and help you achieve wealth.

CHAPTER 10

OVERCOMING OBSTACLES AND CHALLENGES

You've made progress. I'm really excited that you've reached this stage. As you carefully read through each page of this chapter, the purpose of addressing this topic in the section will become clear.

The journey towards success in life is not an easy path. It's filled with twists, turns, and obstacles that challenge our determination and resilience. However, it is through overcoming these challenges that we discover opportunities for growth and transformation.

Times serve as catalysts for development in ways that easy times cannot achieve. By facing obstacles head-on and navigating through them, we strengthen our ability to bounce back from setbacks. Recognizing our capacity to solve problems, learn from hardships, and gain insights from mistakes lays the foundation for success.

Ultimately, encountering and conquering challenges becomes a part of striving for success. How we approach these obstacles ultimately shapes our growth or limits. I know you've heard the phrase, "The fears you face become your limits." Well, guess what? This is something that holds true for challenges as well.

If you don't face the curve ball life through, you won't grow, and you won't excel. Most people think that they already know this and live by it. But, I hate to break it to you: they don't. You see, when most of us face challenges in life, we tend to change our goals and pursue a pursuit that has rather fewer obstacles.

This approach here is not to deal with challenges and obstacles. Those who work with such an approach only achieve the bare minimum and sadly never unlock their true potential in life. However, to live a life that's truly fulfilling, you must be willing to admit that you can and will fail.

But you must also be capable of getting back up after failure, learning from it, tackling the challenges, and achieving your goals. With that in mind, let's look at how you can identify challenges in life.

IDENTIFYING COMMON OBSTACLES AND CHALLENGES

If you think that you are ready for your journey toward success, you need to keep in mind that there may be obstacles and challenges along the way. Each person's path is unique, but that doesn't mean that they won't face any challenges down the road. The key to achieving success is not to avoid challenges but to embrace them as learning opportunities that help us grow.

To overcome the challenges we face, it's important to not only understand why we failed but to use failure as a lesson and find a solution. There are many reasons why people face challenges in life and tend to run away from them. Understanding these reasons will help to change your perspective on challenges and allow you to come up with solutions. Some of these reasons include:

1. **Fear of Failure**

Sometimes, our fear of not succeeding holds us back from taking risks and exploring opportunities. It's important to embrace failure as a part of the learning process, allowing us to move forward with confidence and trust in ourselves.

2. **Self-doubt and Limiting Beliefs**

We often find ourselves thinking, *"I can't do it."* However, it's crucial to question these thoughts. Who decides what we can do or cannot achieve? Negative self-talk and deeply ingrained beliefs can undermine our confidence and self-worth. To overcome these barriers, we must identify them, challenge their validity, and affirm our confidence with positivity.

3. **Lack of Direction**

Feeling lost or without purpose is an experience when we lack clarity and direction in life. Without goals and a sense of purpose, it becomes challenging to make decisions and maintain motivation. Setting goals provides us with a roadmap for success, helping us regain focus and drive.

4. **Procrastination and Lack of Discipline**

Delaying tasks or struggling to stay focused can hinder our progress. By acknowledging these obstacles, understanding how they impact our lives, and adopting strategies to address them, we can pave the way for growth and success. To avoid procrastination, it is essential to improve time management skills and practice self-discipline.

5. Resistance to Change

This is a hurdle we face on the journey to success. Stepping out of our comfort zones and embracing the unknown is essential for growth. However, the resistance to change can hold us back from making adjustments, resulting in our pursuit of success being more challenging than it already is. Being open to learning, unlearning habits, and relearning is crucial in this process.

6. Not Having A Support System

You must understand that a support system plays a major role when striving for success. It can be tough to stay motivated and persevere without the backing of friends, family, or mentors. There are times in life when we need to have a different perspective on life or the challenges we face, and that is just what a support system is for.

7. Financial Limitations

The lack of monetary resources often poses an obstacle when establishing a business or pursuing education. However, exploring financial management approaches or actively seeking funding opportunities can help overcome this hurdle. Remember everything we talked about in the last chapter?

8. Time Constraints

Some of the challenges we face in life require time to be addressed. However, Balancing professional responsibilities often leads to time constraints. To make progress toward success, it's important to prioritize tasks based on their importance and effectively utilize time.

There are a few other things that can make our life more challenging than it really is. Constantly comparing ourselves to others can result in feelings of inadequacy and a loss of confidence. Instead, it's crucial that we shift our focus towards self-improvement and finding satisfaction in our accomplishments.

With renewed hope, you can face each challenge head-on by transforming fear into motivation to persevere. However, it's important to know that all the challenges we face in life can be addressed with a little effort and dedication. We must learn to set goals to guide us through times and establish routines and discipline to avoid the pitfalls of procrastination.

Being resourceful and smart will help you navigate obstacles. You must learn how to prioritize your time and take care of yourself to recharge your energy levels. Seek support from a community that provides connection and strength, reminding you that you don't have to face this journey. Find pride in growth rather than comparing yourself to others.

It's important to understand that identifying challenges in life is not an easy thing to do as our vision and judgment become clouded with fear, lack of confidence, and all the other reasons we've talked about above. To truly overcome challenges in life, you must first determine why you see that particular event as a challenge.

This is something that's oftentimes easier said than done. To effectively answer this question, analyze the challenge based on the factors mentioned above. Are you afraid of it? Do you lack confidence? Are you not able to make the required time? Think about all of these factors and determine why something is challenging.

This will not only help you understand the problem better, but it will also help you come up with relevant and effective solutions that allow you to excel on your journey to success. While challenges may persist, view them as opportunities for growth; they are stepping stones along the way. With consistency and patience, stumbling blocks eventually transform into building blocks.

This journey of a thousand steps gains momentum one day at a time. So, with that in mind, let's look at some key problem-solving strategies that'll help you overcome challenges.

STRATEGIES FOR PROBLEM-SOLVING

When it comes to addressing challenges in life, the first thing that you need to understand is that you won't get anywhere with a stringent approach. These challenges we face in life occur because we're falling short in one area or another. To overcome them, we must acknowledge this and work on improving ourselves by developing a growth mindset.

To develop a growth mindset, it is crucial to take steps towards conquering challenges. Instead of seeing problems as barriers, approach them as opportunities for learning and personal development. Adopting an outlook that encourages growth empowers you to see setbacks as hurdles as opposed to permanent failures, enabling you to devise innovative solutions. Some of the key strategies for problem-solving include:

1. **Understanding the Challenge**

   When faced with a problem, it can be helpful to take a step back and approach it from an outsider's perspective. Break down the challenge into tasks, allowing you to better comprehend its root cause. Once you've done that, the next thing you need to do is explore solutions with a growth mindset.

   Having such a mindset helps us understand the issue at hand and devise a plan to tackle it effectively. Dealing with failure, in a manner, is a part of our journey towards success. It's important for us to develop resilience and bounce back from setbacks, viewing them as opportunities for growth rather than as the end. Embracing our mistakes allows us to learn and shape our approach, fueling our determination to move forward with wisdom.

2. **Seeking Support**

You must remember that seeking support when faced
with a problem is not a sign of weakness but a display of
strength. It's beneficial to reach out to people we know,
such as friends, family members, teachers, or cowork-
ers, for assistance. Gaining perspectives and receiving
support can provide insights and motivation needed to
overcome obstacles. Remember that you don't have to
face tough times all by yourself. Sometimes, we're just
too close to the problem to see it for what it's really
worth.

3. **Building Adaptability and Flexibility**

You must understand that these are essential qualities for success. To thrive in situations, it's essential to
embrace change and remain open-minded about ad-
justing your plans. By being adaptable, you'll be better
equipped to navigate challenges effortlessly by alter-
ing your course when necessary while maintaining a
growth mindset.

4. **Seeking Solutions**

When confronted with challenges – developing problem-solving skills will serve you well on your journey.
To improve your problem-solving skills, it is beneficial
to engage in thinking and explore approaches. This will
equip you with the ability to tackle challenges effortlessly as they arise and will also help you come up with
solutions on a continuous basis.

5. **Having A Positive Attitude**

This is something that can make all the difference when confronted with difficulties. By approaching problems positively, you increase your chances of staying focused, motivated, and finding solutions. It's essential to acknowledge that our mindset plays a role in shaping the outcomes we experience.

Remember that achieving success doesn't mean avoiding challenges. Instead, it requires determination and resilience to overcome them. Regard problems as opportunities for growth and learning, understanding that each obstacle conquered brings you closer to achieving greatness.

With resolve, resilience, and a commitment to development, you possess the capability to overcome any hurdle and attain the level of success you aspire for. Therefore, it is important to confront your problems head-on because by doing you will discover fulfillment in pursuing your dreams and uncover possibilities.

And with that, dear friend, this chapter and this book both come to an end. I would like to take this moment now to congratulate you on choosing this book and finishing it all the way. I am sure you enjoyed the read and found it filled with valuable insight that you can apply in life. I urge you to make great use of the knowledge I have shared with you.

We've started off with learning about what success really means and what it's all about. Then, we transitioned to learning about challenges, mindset, habits, finances, and so much more. We've covered quite a lot in this book. Now, let's just take a quick look back and see how far we've come.

CONCLUSION

You need to understand that every beginning eventually comes to a close. It's important to remember that this isn't the end. It's crucial to take the steps to ensure that the ongoing process continues smoothly. Do you know someone looking for success at every stage?

Tell them to look no further than "Achieving Success at Every Step." This comprehensive and practical guide is perfect for anyone who wants to unlock their potential and excel in all areas of life. Tell them that, throughout our journey, we have explored strategies for overcoming challenges, personal growth, and savoring the taste of victory.

On your journey to excellence, remember that success doesn't happen overnight. It's a process that requires commitment, determination, and a mindset focused on growth by recognizing that success encompasses different aspects that we have defined to improve our understanding. Throughout this book, we learned that we often limit ourselves with negative beliefs and self-doubt.

But we didn't just stop there. We went on to learn that we can overcome these beliefs by changing our perceptions and learning to improve ourselves. We discovered that our minds have to be shaped in such a way that we view failures not as obstacles but as stones toward achieving greatness.

We have acquired knowledge about cultivating habits and effectively managing our time. This enables us to consistently make progress towards our aspirations. With self-discipline and perseverance, we can develop the confidence to confront challenges head-on, knowing that every setback presents an opportunity for growth.

We learned that when it comes to facing challenges, we must first determine why we see the event as a challenge to begin with. To do this, we must analyze our perception of success using different factors, such as the fear of failure and a lack of confidence. Once we have determined why we see an event as a challenge, we can deduce what we need to tackle it.

This helps us identify what we need to work on to overcome the challenge. Throughout this transformative experience, we have deeply grasped the importance of connection and support. We learned to build relationships with mentors we deeply respect, as well as a diverse network that supports our goals and dreams.

These meaningful connections significantly contribute to our growth and propel us toward success. But that's not all. We also learned that seeking help is not a sign of weakness but a display of strength. Moreover, we recognize the importance of balance and overall well-being in sustaining our vitality and ensuring the accomplishment of long-term aspirations.

We also learn that being successful in life doesn't really have anything to do with money. We determined that money is an important aspect of success as it helps remove limitations that may exist due to monetary restrictions. Do you remember we talked about why building a solid financial foundation is necessary?

We even covered budgeting savings and investing practices that help us achieve financial freedom and allow leverage money as a tool for achieving greatness. Do you recall that achieving success is not about reaching a destination but embarking on a personal voyage of growth and fulfillment?

It remains a pursuit where each small step brings us closer to greatness. Then, fixating on the final goal, it is crucial to embrace and appreciate the transformative process itself—the knowledge gained, relationships formed, and pure joy experienced. Let's embark together on this journey by applying the advice and techniques discovered within these pages.

Together, we can cultivate a mindset aimed at achieving success; have the courage to envision your dreams and take steps towards realizing them. As we contemplate the possibilities that lie ahead, let us always remember that success is within our grasp.

Let's embrace personal growth and always seek opportunities to learn and grow, and work towards achieving our goals. Remember that those who fearlessly pursue success will eventually achieve greatness.

As we near the end of this book on success, we are not bidding farewell to the journey we started. Instead, we are embracing an adventure. The wisdom gained from these pages will always be with us, guiding us through life's ups and downs.

It serves as the cornerstone that we can use to base our perception, decision-making, and efforts, which will indeed propel us in the right direction, allowing us to achieve greatness, fulfillment, and success in each and every aspect of life!

Dear friend, I wish you the best of luck on the journey you started with me. May you achieve all that you want and become all that you strive to be!

Good Luck!

CHAPTER
"GOOD WILL"

Helping others without expectation of anything in return has been proven to lead to increased happiness and satisfaction in life.

I would love to give you the chance to experience that same feeling during your reading or listening experience today...

All it takes is a few moments of your time to answer one simple question:

<u>Would you make a difference in the life of someone you've never met—without spending any money or seeking recognition for your good will?</u>

If so, I have a small request for you.

If you've found value in your reading or listening experience today, I humbly ask that you take a brief moment right now to leave an honest review of this book. It won't cost you anything but 30 seconds of your time—just a few seconds to share your thoughts with others.

Your voice can go a long way in helping someone else find the same inspiration and knowledge that you have.

Are you familiar with leaving a review for an Audible, Kindle, or e-reader book? If so, it's simple:

If you're on **Audible**: just hit the three dots in the top right of your device, click rate & review, then leave a few sentences about the book along with your star rating.

If you're reading on **Kindle** or an e-reader, simply scroll to the last page of the book and swipe up—the review should prompt from there.

If you're on a **Paperback** or any other physical format of this book, you can find the book page on Amazon (or wherever you bought this) and leave your review right there.

ABOUT THE AUTHOR

This author has a knack for capturing the essence of life's complexities, intricacies, and universal truths through her writing, often presenting thought-provoking perspectives on various aspects of existence. Her life books are characterized by rich character development, as the author skillfully weaves together the stories of diverse topics, illuminating journeys, challenges, and triumphs. Through books, the author explores themes such as love, passion, victory, identity, personal growth, and the search for meaning, offering readers profound insights and moments of introspection.

Beyond Zoë's professional accomplishments, she also has a rich and multifaceted life outside of publishing. This book is a testament to her commitment to providing valuable insights and practical guidance. The author's books are often praised for their ability to evoke empathy in readers, fostering a deep connection between the readers and the valuable insights they encounter within the pages.

The author is a distinguished authority in various fields of study, bringing a wealth of knowledge and experience to her thought-provoking non-fiction works. As you delve into Zoë's manuscripts, you can expect to embark on an intellectual journey guided by Zoë's profound insights and intentional thought-provoking passion for self -development. Her non-fiction works continue to push the boundaries of knowledge, inviting readers to expand their horizons and gain a deeper understanding of life and its impact on our success.

Zoë's works have been praised for their meticulous research, insightful analysis, and the way they challenge readers to think critically about the world around them.

Any one of Zoë's latest book,....

1. **Unlocking Infinity: Master the Art of Longevity**

    Learn How to, Boost Your Brain Health, Recharge Your Immune System and Restore Youthful Balance in 3 Easy Steps

2. **Living Your Best Life: Radiate from Within**

    Ultimate Guide to Finding Purpose & Fulfillment in 3 Easy Steps.

3. **Redefining Aging: The Art of Living Alone**

    How to Find Joy in Independence, Live Fearlessly & Maintain Longevity

4. **Longevity: The Art of Aging Backwards**

    Step-by-Step Guide to Renew, Restore and Reverse Aging Mentally, Physically & Spiritually

5. **Journeying Alone, Journeying Strong: Navigating Aging Alone Without Children**

Self-Help Guide to Finding Inner Strength, Peace, Joy & Fulfillment in Childless Aging

6. **Alone, But Not Lonely: Aging on Your Terms**

A Roadmap for Aging Independently, Striking Balance & Finding Purpose

7. **The Positivity Code: Supercharge Your Life with Positive Thinking**

Learn The Art of Positive Thinking, Changing Your Life One Thought at a Time

8. **The Growth Mindset Code: Cracking the Secrets to Success**

Comprehensive Guide to Breaking Limits with A Growth Mindset, Cultivating Unlimited Possibilities

9. **The Superfood Prescription: Refuel Your Mind & Body**

100 Supercharged Foods to Revitalize & Transform Your Health

... is another testament to her dedication to delivering enlightening and captivating non-fiction literature. Whether you're a seasoned reader of non-fiction or new to the genre Zoë's work is sure to engage, inform, and inspire.

To stay updated on **Zoë Publishing's** latest projects and musings, visit us on **facebook.com/zoepublishing** and follow us on Instagram & Tik Tok (**@zoepublishing**)

REFERENCES

Covey, S. R. (1989). The 7 habits of highly effective people. New York: Simon & Schuster.

Christensen, C. M. (2015). *The innovator's dilemma: When New Technologies Cause Great Firms to Fail*. Harvard Business Review Press.

Dweck, C. S. (2006). Mindset: The new psychology of success. New York: Ballantine Books.

Eat that frog & start accomplishing your goals | Brian Tracy. (2022, September 7). Brian Tracy. https://www.briantracy.com/blog/time-management/the-truth-about-frogs/

Eisenhower Matrix. (2022, March 10). Prioritization Framework | Definition and Examples. https://www.productplan.com/glossary/eisenhower-matrix/

Ericsson, K. A., & Pool, R. (2016). Peak: Secrets from the new science of expertise. Boston: Houghton Mifflin Harcourt.

Fontinelle, A. (2022). How to set financial goals for your future. *Investopedia*. https://www.investopedia.com/articles/personal-finance/100516/setting-financial-goals/

Frankl, V. E. (1946). Man's search for meaning. Boston: Beacon Press.

Gladwell, M. (2008). Outliers: The story of success. New York: Little, Brown and Company.

Gladwell, M. (2022). *The tipping point: How Little Things Can Make a Big Difference*. Hachette UK.

Goleman, D. (1995). Emotional intelligence. New York: Bantam Books.

Hayes, A. (2023). Investment Basics Explained With Types to Invest in. *Investopedia*. https://www.investopedia.com/terms/i/investment.asp

Hill, N. (1937). Think and grow rich. Meriden, CT: The Ralston Society.

Maxwell, J. C. (1998). The 21 irrefutable laws of leadership: Follow them and people will follow you. Nashville: Thomas Nelson Publishers.

McGonigal, K. (2015). The Upside of Stress: Why Stress Is Good for You, and How to Get Good at It. New York: Avery Publishing Group.

MindTools | Home. (n.d.). https://www.mindtools.com/a4wo118/smart-goals

Newport, C. (2016). Deep work: Rules for focused success in a distracted world. New York: Grand Central Publishing.

Pant, P. (2022, June 20). What is the difference between wants and needs? *The Balance*. https://www.thebalance-money.com/how-to-separate-wants-and-needs-453592

Picardo, E. (2022). Investing Explained: Types of Investments and How To Get Started. *Investopedia*. https://www.investopedia.com/terms/i/investing.asp

Pink, D. H. (2009). Drive: The surprising truth about what motivates us. New York: Riverhead Books.

Robert. (2023). How To Prioritize With The ABCDE Method. *Time Hack Hero*. https://timehackhero.com/the-abc-de-method-to-do-list-priority/

Schwahn, L. (2023). How to Budget for Short-Term and Long-Term Financial Goals. *NerdWallet*. https://www.nerd-wallet.com/article/finance/short-vs-long-term-goals

Sinek, S. (2009). Start with why: How great leaders inspire everyone to take action. New York: Portfolio/Penguin.

Sweller, J., Ayres, P., & Kalyuga, S. (2011). *Cognitive Load Theory*. Springer Science & Business Media.

The complete guide to time blocking. (n.d.). Todoist. https://todoist.com/productivity-methods/time-blocking

Time Management - Pareto, ABC & Co. (n.d.). https://www.landsiedel.com/en/coaching/time-management.html

Yasar, K. (2022). SMART (SMART goals). *WhatIs.com*. https://www.techtarget.com/whatis/definition/SMART-SMART-goals